## ABOUT THE AUTHOR

Steve Swanson is a man of many talents. As a student at St. Olaf College in Northfield, Minn., he combined excellence in studies with football. Following college, he attended seminary, and after his ordination he served churches in Minnesota, Oregon, and Saskatoon, Saskatchewan.

At the University of Oregon, Texas Lutheran College, and Camrose Lutheran College he doubled as professor of English and coach of wrestling, football, volleyball, and hockey.

He has worked as bulldozer operator, carpenter, cabinetmaker, hod carrier, hay farmer, roofer, auto body man, auto and tractor mechanic, plumber, and trucker.

Steve enjoys restoring old cars, remodeling houses, and building boats in Northfield where he has lived since 1974 with his wife Judy and their four children. He teaches English at St. Olaf College, serves area churches, and keeps busy writing articles and books.

# Bible Readings
# FOR
# MEN

# Bible Readings

# FOR
# MEN

•

## Steve Swanson

**AUGSBURG** Publishing House • Minneapolis

**BIBLE READINGS FOR MEN**

**Library of Congress Cataloging in Publication Data**

Swanson, Stephen O.
  BIBLE READINGS FOR MEN.

  1. Men—Prayer-books and devotions—English.  I. Title.
BV4843.S9  1984        242'.642        83-72116
ISBN 0-8066-2060-9 (pbk.)

Manufactured in the U.S.A.                         APH 10-0682

1  2  3  4  5  6  7  8  9  0  1  2  3  4  5  6  7  8  9

*For Cully, my father,*
*and for all other good men*
*who are faithful examples to their children*
*and to the world*

# PREFACE

Never in the history of God's dealings with humankind has there been more need for active, informed, concerned, and faithful men. As the nuclear family breaks down, as our heads swirl with the ups and downs of a sexual revolution, as women move into areas and activities that we always thought were "ours," we feel more and more threatened, more and more concerned about what it means to be a man.

The most important resource book that speaks to that concern is the Bible. The Old Testament is the story of a patriarchal society; it is largely about men—patriarchs, kings and their courtiers, prophets, judges, soldiers—men of faith, men of vision—men with weaknesses to be sure, but men who spoke to God and to whom God spoke.

The New Testament is also a book about a man and his men: Jesus and his 12 followers—and their followers, both men and women, who went out in the name of Christ and changed the world.

The church of Christ still needs men and needs them desperately. This little book is dedicated to that need. By reading it we hope you will become stronger in faith, be a better churchman, a better father, a better husband, a better friend, a better employer or employee, a better citizen, and more. God bless you as you read and think and pray and more and more become a man of God.

# ■ LIFE ISN'T FAIR

Eccles. 9:1-6: "All share a common destiny—
the righteous and the wicked, the good and the
bad . . . " (v. 2).

Sometimes it takes an older person to come up with
a bit of wisdom at the right time. Ken Collins was
finishing his research project and starting to write up
the results in report form, a report he hoped would
get him a bonus, a raise, and maybe advancement, too.
Then he saw an article in a trade journal announcing
the same breakthrough in a rival company.

"They'll get the patent, and I'll get chewed out for
not working faster," Ken said to Bill Browne, the lab's
senior researcher. "Life isn't fair."

"Life has never been fair," Bill said. "Just read the
Bible, for heaven's sake." Bill and Ken often talked
religion. They had a faith in common, and that often
drew them together at lunch hour and on breaks to
discuss religion in general or the moral implications
of their current research projects. "Look at Adam and
Eve; look at Job; look at Uriah, the most faithful
soldier in David's army."

"I know, but I really worked hard; I really wanted
this one."

"The most important things we don't even have to
work for," Bill said.

Ken smiled a thank-you. He needed that reminder,
and from someone like Bill, who had been through
so much, it meant a lot.

 Lord, help me keep life's smaller
disappointments in perspective.

**Nothing is a complete loss. There is experience, there
is learning, there is growth, even in the most
disappointing events.**

11

# ■ BEING PLEASANT

Prov. 8:32-36:  "Blessed is the man who listens to me . . . " (v. 34).

A man can't just decide to be pleasant overnight. Sometimes half a lifetime of being moody or even grumpy gets in the way. The overnight reform of Scrooges happens only in stories. We need a philosophy of pleasantness and a place to start.

The philosophy goes back to Christ himself: "Love one another," Jesus said. Pleasantness is one of the mild and genial ways we show that love.

Without love, pleasantness becomes difficult. We all know people who profess great faith and who talk a good line of religion but who are so grumpy that they turn off others left and right.

Pleasantness is a logical place and a useful way to start professing our faith. "Why is he always so pleasant?" people will ask. "How come he always whistles?" "How can he smile when so much is going wrong?"

"Maybe it's his religion," people will answer. "Maybe it's because he's so active in his church."

Knowing what Christ has done for us, knowing how highly he has valued us, and knowing of the eternal places he has prepared for us should keep a smile on our faces most of the time.

 Lord, make me a happy person. Heal the hurts in my life and make me smile.

**Happiness is contagious. If you are troubled with grumpiness, start hanging around with some happy people.**

# ■ BREAKING THE ROUTINE

Jer. 31:23-25: "I will refresh the weary and satisfy the faint" (v. 25).

Louis and Suzanne Colburn sat in their usual after-supper chairs reading their usual magazines and, as usual, not saying much. Louis laid down his magazine and stared into space for a long while, then suddenly said, almost too loudly, "I'm bored."

"Bored? Bored with me or what?" Suzanne asked.

"Bored with routine, I think. We do—or at least I do —everything the same every day. I get up, eat breakfast, ride to work in the same car pool, sit at the same desk, eat at the same cafe, come home, eat, sit here, go to bed, get up."

"Tomorrow's Saturday," Suzanne said. "Suppose we have an antiroutine weekend. We'll have supper for breakfast, breakfast for supper, midnight snack for lunch, and spend the day in the library."

"A Saturday in the library?"

"Sure. And Sunday we'll visit as many church services as we can in one morning."

"You're on. And Monday I'll ride my bike to work."

Lord, remind me that most of life and work are routine, but teach me to fight its boredom.

There is usually no need to change jobs or towns or to give up on our marriage; we just need to restructure our routines.

13

# ■ GETTING OUT OF A SLUMP

Lam. 3:52-57: "I called on your name, O Lord, from the depths of the pit" (v. 55).

Don Carpenter walked over and flicked off the TV in disgust. He had been watching a baseball player discuss his hitting slump on the morning sportscast. "He should talk about a slump," Don said to his roommate. "I've been in a slump for a whole year."

"I haven't even known you for a year," his roommate chuckled. "You don't seem too slumpy to me."

"Well, I am. I was going along so well, getting raises, being offered new territories, getting along with Myrna—now everything has stopped. I'm stagnant. Stuck. Mired."

"Here, grab this, I'll pull you out." Don's roommate had flipped a dish towel to him like a lifeline.

It *was* a lifeline. They laughed. They talked.

Don's roommate suggested a vocational counselor he had once consulted. Don had taken the first step toward better times.

Lord, thank you for my friends, who help me out of slumps. Make me such a friend, too.

**Often a slump is merely a mire in the mind. The love of Christ can reach into that mire and pull us out.**

# ■ WHO ARE MY ROLE MODELS?

Ps. 147:1-11: "His pleasure is not in the strength of the horse, nor his delight in the legs of a man" (v. 10).

Dan Siegel turned off the TV at 1:30 A.M. Glued to an old John Wayne movie he had seen as a kid, he wondered how that movie had influenced his life. He wondered about others of his early role models. He was too sleepy to pursue the question.

Next morning Dan sat down and made a list. He started with John Wayne and listed a few other movie stars, all *macho* types, *except* one singer-comedian. He added to the list a couple of presidents and several athletes.

"Weird list," he said to himself. "I'm none of those people anymore. Probably never was. Who really has influenced my life?"

He listed his father, two of his uncles, a couple of pastors, and some people whom he had never seen but had read about: Bonhoeffer, Gandhi, C. S. Lewis, and others—and Jesus. Especially Jesus.

Dan Siegel's role models had changed. He had given up most of the violence and speed and recklessness of his youth. He had become a gentle man—like those piston ring signs he used to see as a kid: "Tough, but oh, so gentle." Dan Siegel thanked God for the change.

 O Lord, continue to dissolve my violence and my anger. Teach me to show strength in gentleness.

**Thinking back to our youth, wasn't it usually the biggest and strongest boys who were the gentlest? The knowledge of strength is the beginning of gentleness.**

15

# ■ NATURE, A MIRACLE OF SEASONS

Ps. 104:14-23: "The moon marks off the seasons . . ." (v. 19).

Most of us are seasonal people. We tune in to nature's promises and warnings and live our lives seasonally. We feel the deep heat of those early summer days and decide to put on the last two or three screens. We slow down a bit on the hottest summer afternoons and don't mind the thought of autumn at all.

When autumn threatens us with its crisp nights and just a hint of that now-forbidden smell of burning leaves, we begin to batten down and nail down and caulk up for winter.

Winter is again a slow-down time, when nature and people both go dormant. Winter is a time of waiting— warming and waiting.

But spring awakens new hope and new opportunity. The cycle of life renews itself and promises yet another year, another panorama of seasons.

We need not wonder that God, in infinite wisdom, set Easter in the early spring, the season of life anew, the season of life forever.

 Lord, show me the cycles also in my life. Renew me again and again to praise and serve you.

**Seeing our lives as seasonal gives us permission to take up and lay down short-term challenges and opportunities.**

# ■ REMEMBERING TO BE HUMBLE

Mic. 6:6-8: "And what does the Lord require of you? To act justly and to love mercy and to walk humbly with your God" (v. 8).

When the board announced that Will was to be the new president of Southwest Petroleum, he was elated, he was ecstatic, he was just bursting with pride. In his mind he outlined his upward route: he had been trained—and trained well—in geology. He had taken seriously his early years of field work, supervising drilling crews and exploring new fields with seismic crews. He had studied business management and economics on his own. When five years earlier he was invited to join the company's many vice-presidents, he was ready.

Will drove home that afternoon with these many accomplishments still running through his mind like a circular repeat tape. Then suddenly he said to himself, "I've forgotten God. I'm sitting here giving myself all the credit, and I have absolutely forgotten God."

From that moment Will began to look more humbly at his accomplishments. He reminded himself of all the answered prayers that had helped him achieve his goals: his health, a loving and supportive wife, a stable family and home, cooperative colleagues. He could go on and on. Without God's love and help and providence he could have done nothing.

Will drove the rest of the way home alternately whistling "Praise God from whom all blessings flow," and smiling from ear to ear. Other drivers must have thought him wacky.

Make me humble, O Lord. Drown my pride in thankfulness.

**A Christian's successes are mostly God's.**

# ■ THE SIMPLE LIFE—AND THE COMPLEX

Isa. 32:14-20:  "My people will live in peaceful dwelling places, in secure homes . . ." (v. 18).

When Ann and Ernie invited the Williamsons back for a neighborhood dinner, they were tingling with anticipation. This was the Williamson's first time back in the neighborhood after six months of their new life on the farm.

The Williamsons had sold their house, left the suburban neighborhood, and tried a simpler kind of life. Alec Williamson cut his job back to part-time; his wife, who had been weaving church vestments, altar cloths, and banners for years, now began to turn that hobby into her vocation.

Ann and Ernie and the other neighbors were anxious to hear all this. Some had believed secretly that the Williamsons wouldn't make it, but all had wished them well.

The visit was a marvelous success. The Williamsons had found real joy in their struggle, and that spilled over to the neighbors. Not only Ann and Ernie, but several others as well went home that night and talked about simplifying their lives. No one moved to a farm, no one quit any job, but they did simplify in a variety of ways. The Williamsons had set an important example.

 Lord, help me to see where my life is too complex. Then help me to simplify.

**The fringe benefit of a simplified life is time. Those who live close to the earth seem to have a bit more time.**

# ■ HOW MANY THINGS DO I NEED?

Luke 12:13-21: "A man's life does not consist in
the abundance of his possessions" (v. 15).

The wish book," Jerry said out loud.

"What?" Lily asked from the kitchen sink.

"That's what grandma and grandpa used to call this
catalog—the wish book." Jerry thought back to his
childhood and grandfather's farm and the
well-thumbed mail-order catalogs stacked on top of an
old cabinet in the kitchen.

"We've lost our wishes," he said to himself. "We
are so well off that we don't even dream. We just buy
whatever we need." He looked once again at the
popcorn poppers in the catalog, then looked around
the kitchen. He couldn't see the garbage disposal
under the sink, but he knew it was there. He couldn't
see the electric can opener, the food processor and
mixer, the toaster, the electric frying pan, and the
waffle iron, but he knew they were there. The range
he could see, as well as a two-door refrigerator, and a
dishwasher.

He thought of the mission film he'd seen at church
last week showing women hunkered down, cooking
wheat cakes on a rock heated by a fire. Jerry was
suddenly ashamed. "I guess we really don't need a
corn popper," he said. "We've been popping good
corn in that old pan for years." He paused only briefly
before asking Lily, "What did you do with that world
hunger mailing that came last week?"

 Lord, make us content. Let us not be distracted,
drowned, or damned by things.

**Sales resistance usually starts with small decisions and
ends in more important ones—so do decisions about
stewardship.**

# ■ JEALOUSY ON THE JOB

Gen. 26:12-16: "He had so many flocks and herds and servants that the Philistines envied him" (v. 14).

When Adolf Brown, the store manager, hired an outsider, John Fenster, to be his new assistant manager, everyone knew that John was being groomed to manage the new store on Capitol Drive. At least four of the department managers secretly wanted that job and were jealous of John. They didn't work very well with him, either, and they went out of their way to make it tough for him. It took John Fenster at least two months longer to learn the ins and outs of the business because of the envy and hostility of many of the regular staff.

One man, Carl Dorlie, decided right away to work with John Fenster instead of against him. Carl decided it wasn't John's fault that he and the others were bypassed for the assistant manager's post. Carl helped when the others refused; he befriended John and helped him learn. But it also cost him some hard times with the others. At morning coffee a few of the regulars wouldn't even sit with Carl any more.

In six months John Fenster left to manage the new store, and things were pretty much back to normal. A year later Adolph Brown decided to take early retirement. He remembered how Carl had befriended John and recommended that the board hire Carl as his own replacement. Carl and John now have a good working relationship managing the sister stores.

 Lord, help me to be a more friendly and accepting person. Teach me to be happy at the success of others.

**Jealousy and envy have a boomerang effect. They hurt us more than they hurt those of whom we are jealous.**

# ■ WANTING RECOGNITION

Matt. 20:20-28: " 'What is it you want?' he asked.
She said, 'Grant that one of these two sons of mine
may sit at your right and the other at your left in your
kingdom' " (v. 21).

For many of us life has been a constant quest for
recognition. It started when we were boys playing
baseball or soccer or singing solos in church. Our
parents may have reinforced our feelings by
recognizing and encouraging every instance of our
efforts and performances.

You'd think that living a life of faith as adults would
mean we could completely avoid striving so hard
for recognition. Humility, after all, is one of the
cardinal virtues and by now should have overcome
our desire to be singled out.

The episode with James and John and their mother
reminds us that even those closest to Jesus were
constantly jockeying for position and recognition. We
shouldn't be surprised, then, that pride and desire for
recognition and reward are a constant component of
*our* everyday lives.

But we can engrave in our memories the way Jesus
handled the mother's request: "Whoever wants to
become great among you must be your servant, and
whoever wants to be first must be your slave"
(Matt. 20:26-27).

 Lord, let our pride be in you and our joy be in
serving others.

**Sometimes we are happier and might be further
ahead in the long run by being supporters, helpers,
and followers of others.**

# ■ I'M NOT TRAINED FOR THAT JOB

Exod. 4:10-16: "Moses said to the Lord, 'O Lord, I have never been eloquent, neither in the past nor since you have spoken to your servant. I am slow of speech and tongue'" (v. 10).

We've heard a lot about the Peter Principle in the last decade, and we know it does work that way sometimes. People can get promoted to the level of their incompetence, and the wise employee knows when to stick tight and refuse a promotion—no matter how pleased the person is to have been offered the job.

God asked Moses to be a great leader. Moses didn't see himself that way and tried to refuse, claiming he didn't have the skills necessary for the job. God took care of that. He reassured Moses and quieted his fears by also enlisting Moses' brother Aaron. Aaron was to be the spokesman for Moses.

When opportunities for advancement come our way, we can wisely and with prayer try to assess the challenges of the job, measuring them against our own training and skills and adaptability. God and God's Word can help us see ourselves honestly so that we can avoid wrong choices and move boldly when the time is right.

 Lord, please help me make wise choices in times of tough decision.

**Seeing ourselves as God sees us can give us courage to say either yes or no to a vocational opportunity and live with our decision.**

# ■ GETTING ALONG WITH THE BOSS

1 Sam. 18:10-11: "Saul had a spear in his hand and he hurled it, saying to himself, 'I'll pin David to the wall' " (v. 11).

What surprises us is that David dodged Saul's spear *twice*. David knew Saul was sick; he knew the king was subject to depressions and fits of rage and jealousy. He stayed around for Saul's second shot.

David sets us an example in getting along with a difficult leader, a difficult boss or foreman. The ideal executive is one who gets the best people he or she can find, gives them direction and authority, and then praises them for the good job they do.

Not every boss is like that. The good job some employees do threatens some bosses. They see their jobs, their authority, and their very beings teetering. Then they begin to act like Saul.

No one, not even God, expects us to stay around to dodge every spear neurotic employers might hurl at us, but we can learn to dodge many of the words and much of the anger and peevishness they may dump on us. We can learn to understand, befriend, and help employers even as we continue to do our jobs well. The love of Christ can teach us these skills.

 Lord, make me a wise and understanding employee.

**Talking to other employees about supporting and working with the boss can sometimes ease tensions for everyone.**

# ■ BLAMING OTHERS

Gen. 3:6-12: "The man said, 'The woman you put here with me — she gave me some fruit from the tree, and I ate'" (v. 12).

W hen Charlie Peters crunched the fender of the family station wagon, he blamed his wife Ruth.

"You shouldn't have told me to look at that helicopter," he said to her.

"You shouldn't have looked when you did."

"How was I to know that car was going to pull out?"

"I don't know. But when *you* are driving, *you* have to watch where *you're* going."

When it comes to driving, everyone in the car should be on the lookout for trouble, but Ruth was right nevertheless. Charlie drove into the other car; Charlie was to blame.

Adam blamed not only Eve. He even blamed God. "The woman *you* put here with me," he said. God gave him a flawed creature, someone to tempt him; and that's why he sinned.

Blaming others for our own mistakes has been a common trait from the begining of human history. Adam did it; we do it. It doesn't do much good, really. However, confession *does* do good and so does apology—and recognizing and accepting our own mistakes so we can learn from them. God is always ready to forgive.

 Lord, make me honest about my own failures and less apt to blame others.

**If you have been blaming someone else for something that was really your own fault, it's time to be honest with yourself—and with that other person, too.**

# ■ NOT A CHANCE

Matt. 10:26-31: "And even the very hairs of your head are all numbered" (v. 30).

The world seems out of control. So many things happen by accident and chance in this world that sometimes we wonder if anyone out there is still running it.

Ask any group of men about experiences of chance, of once-in-a-million, couldn't-be-repeated experiences, and you'll get some stories. A fisherman will tell you how he hooked a lost fishing rod through the end eyelet while trolling. A hunter will tell about the time when, just for a joke, he took a shot at a blackbird on a telephone wire from the back of a moving pickup truck — and hit it. There will be stories of narrow escapes, found treasure, chance meetings.

We wonder, with all this apparent chance and luck (both good and bad), if God has turned the world and its people loose to work out their own destinies.

We have to answer no. The sparrow's fall is noted by God. Both the short- and the long-term futures of this world are in God's control. Our problem is that we can't always see God's plan in the short-term effects. We don't know what God has in mind when chance and even accidents are allowed to change the course of our lives. But we can still trust God.

 Lord, no matter what happens, remind me every day that you are in control.

**Sometimes when we are trying the hardest to control our lives, some weird chance reminds us that we are not captains of our own fates.**

# ■ THE CRAB RING

Phil. 3:12-16: "Forgetting what is behind and straining toward what is ahead, I press on toward the goal . . ." (v. 13).

On his Florida holiday Stan Schwartz planned to walk the beaches and think hard and long about advancement and upward mobility. He wasn't getting along in his company very fast, and he wondered why.

Part of the answer came to him on a fishing pier as he watched an old man tending several crab rings. When a ring was being pulled up, Stan noticed that the netting was tied around two hoops, a larger one on top and a smaller, baited one on the bottom. He could see that when the contraption sank to the bottom it would lie flat so that crabs could then crawl over the netting toward the bait. But when pulled, the larger ring would suddenly come up around the crabs like an inverted cone.

"But why don't they swim out the top?" Stan asked the old man. "The whole top is wide open."

"A crab ring works," said the old man, "because crabs can only swim backwards and sideways."

Stan walked away reflecting on his work back home. "I've been too timid," he said. "Backwards and sideways—that's me." He had a very visible smile on his face as he thought, *That's how crabs get into hot water!*

 Lord, give me flexibility of mind and of movement. Teach me to see opportunity and give me courage to move toward it.

**Flexibility is only as good as any given decision to move. Faith and prayer are the stuff of courageous and wise decisions.**

# ■ A SQUARE PEG

Ps. 9:1-10: "The Lord is a refuge for the oppressed, a stronghold in times of trouble" (v. 9).

Bill Quist's Uncle Eric emigrated from Sweden and worked as an industrial carpenter and cabinetmaker all his life. Years after his uncle's death, Bill's Aunt Millie gave most of his tools to the family. When everything else was spoken for, Bill asked for the weird and mysterious pieces that were left.

Some of the leftover tools he identified from old hardware catalogs, but most baffling of all was a quarter-inch thick steel bar about six inches long and two inches wide, with a row of smaller and smaller holes down the middle. The inside of the holes had sharp V-notches or teeth, except for the last hole, which was smooth.

Bill finally took the tool to a retired cabinetmaker. "Watch," he said, clamping the bar tightly in a vise, flat side up. Then, starting with a short square stick, he hammered it through the largest hole. The teeth sheared off the corners. He hammered it through hole after hole; it became smaller and smaller, until the last hole took off the tooth marks and left the piece smooth and round. Bill's bar was a dowel maker.

Hard and troubled times become for Christians a kind of dowel maker. In the midst of the anger or pain or sorrow that comes from being forced through rough places, we sometimes don't even notice that we are being trimmed into more useful shapes, into more rounded and useful persons.

 Lord, help me learn from troubles and hard times.

**Helping each other through difficult experiences is one way God blesses us in times of trouble.**

# THE FEAR OF CHANGE

Acts 6:8-15: "We have heard him say that this Jesus of Nazareth will destroy this place and change the customs Moses handed down to us" (v. 14).

Change is always scary. The leaders of the synagogues were so frightened of religious change that they killed Deacon Stephen rather than face that change.

We aren't apt to do anything so drastic, but often we do fear change. Many a business and industry is changing right now, and the retraining, reshuffling, and rewriting of job descriptions is scary. But the nature of life and work is change.

One of the classic examples of resistance to change in modern times has been the railroad industry. By protecting jobs at all cost, by holding to the old ways, the railroad passenger industry virtually destroyed itself—and railroad freight isn't far behind.

How do we face change? How do we float with it, learn from it? How do we stride into the high-tech, computer age with confidence? We walk with the Lord.

"Yesterday, today, forever, Jesus is the same," the old hymn says. Some jobs will disappear; some unemployment will result; there will be hardships. But faith in Christ builds faith in ourselves. Somewhere there is for each of us a place to be, a place to work, a place to earn.

 Lord, give me confidence in the face of change. Guide my vocational decisions.

**The time to retrain and prepare for different work is *before* need—like now.**

# ■ HELPING OTHERS BRINGS BLESSINGS

Matt. 25:31-46: "I tell you the truth, whatever you did for one of the least of these brothers of mine, you did for me" (v. 40).

Sylvan Smith is middle-aged now and has been helping people all his life. Someone asked him how he got to be so helpful, so caring. He said it started back in high school. He lived in the Midwest at that time and drove an old Model A Ford to school. One winter day he saw a man lying on a slippery sidewalk. He stopped the car, ran over to the man, and spoke to him.

"Just help me get on my feet," the man said. His breath would have pickled herring.

Sylvan did more than that; he helped the man into the Model A and drove him home to a shabby little dwelling a few blocks away. When he had helped him to the front door, the man turned and quietly said, "God bless you."

Sylvan has received many blessings from many people over the years, but he still chokes up when he thinks of the blessing wished him in his youth by that unfortunate old man. That incident, that blessing got him started.

God promises us blessing for helping others. It is the loving work of Christ to help others—because in helping others, it says in the Bible, we are helping Christ himself.

 Lord, help me to see your image in others, especially those most in need.

**Learning to live the helpful and caring life usually begins just around the corner, as nearby as the next bench, the next desk, next door.**

# ■ UNDERCURRENTS OF ANGER

Eph. 4:25-32: "Get rid of all bitterness, rage, and anger, brawling and slander, along with every form of malice" (v. 31).

Jerry buttoned his shirt and wondered how he had gotten to this point. The doctor had looked at all the tests, asked a lot of questions, and now they were talking about stress.

Jerry knew his wasn't ordinary stress. He had a job he liked, and he was allowed to do it at his own speed and with little pressure. He was happy at home, too, and had few problems in his family life. Yet the tests all showed he was under stress, and he knew that there had to be a reason for it.

Jerry's doctor suggested he see a counselor or his pastor. Jerry made appointments for a few sessions. What those talks uncovered was anger: repressed, pushed down, seething anger. It was because of the sale of the family farm. Many, many suns had gone down on that anger. Jerry thought it was all forgotten: the unfairness of the will and the insensitivity of his brother to how unfair that settlement really was.

Jerry had some things to work out in his family and he had some things to work out in himself. He and his pastor talked and they prayed and Jerry saw better what he had to do. He asked for a week's leave of absence and bought a ticket home. He and his brother would settle some things. Jerry's anger was at last scheduled for a real cure.

 Lord, help me to uncover inside myself those hidden stresses that trouble my life and my health.

**Problems never faced, never cured, never really go away.**

# ■ PATIENCE IS A VIRTUE

Heb. 6:13-20: "And so after waiting patiently,
Abraham received what was promised" (v. 15).

Whenever Al Anders gets impatient, he thinks back
to junior high and his 1918 Evinrude outboard motor.
A neighbor gave it to him back when hardly anyone
was saving antiques. Al took it to the lake that summer
and put it on an old rowboat.

The motor was heavy, all brass and cast iron, and
it started with a knob on top—or at least it was
supposed to start. Al knew before he ever pushed off
from shore that whenever he wanted a ride in that old
boat he could count on a long siege of cranking—10
minutes, 20 minutes, he never knew. All he knew was
that if he wanted to putt-putt around the bay, he had
to crank. He learned patience that summer.

Patience is usually a virtue in the Bible. Simeon
and Anna waited in the temple for the Christ child;
Abraham and Sarah waited for their child of promise.
Faith goes with waiting, faith in the promise.

God has promised to bless us. There are days and
seasons when we have trouble remembering that.
Then we ask for more faith, more patience—and keep
on cranking.

 Lord, give me patience and faith to carry on.

**Sometimes taking a moment to remember the painful
lessons of youth can help us face more mature
challenges.**

# THE REAL CHURCH

John 2:13-22:   "Destroy this temple, and I will raise it again in three days" (v. 19).

While Pastor Carl Orlen was serving his first parish in Upper Michigan, a teenager destroyed his church. The young fellow was tearing around town before dawn one Sunday morning and lost control of his car, knifing it between two trees and right through the side of the church. When the dust settled, the car was completely inside the sanctuary. Pews, Bibles, and hymnbooks had flown everywhere. The boy was unhurt, but the car was badly damaged, and the church now sported a walk-out wall.

When people came to church a few hours later, they were dumbfounded. They just stood around shaking their heads and whispering, as if someone important had died right before their eyes.

Later that week an engineer warned that the roof might fall in or the car might go through the floor if they tried to remove it. A demolition crew tore the building down around the car.

In such a freak accident a church can indeed be destroyed. Arson, too, or accidental fire or windstorms can destroy a church. It isn't rebuilt in three days, either. But there is another church, a church that has no building, a church that cannot be destroyed in these ways. That is the church Jesus spoke of, the church in the heart. No accident, no hurricane, no windstorm, no fire can destroy that church.

 Protect the church in my heart with your Holy Spirit, O Lord.

**Your activity in and love for your visible church will strengthen the invisible church within you.**

# ■ SHARING LOVE

Luke 15:11-32: "Your brother has come . . . and your father has killed the fattened calf . . ." (v. 27).

The parable of the prodigal son touches us all because it measures a father's love. Most kids think their parents don't have quite enough love to go around, so when a prodigal acts up, that somehow demands more love from the parents and sucks the pool dry for the rest of the family. Those feelings go way beyond childhood.

That's what was eating the prodigal's brother. He had been faithful, he had stayed home, he had behaved—but the feast was for the prodigal. "You never gave a feast for me," he said. "Son, you are always with me," the father replied. But words like those don't say "I love you" like a feast, a robe, or a ring on the finger.

A baby will die more surely from lack of love than from lack of food. From infancy on, every member of every family measures himself or herself against the others with love's yardstick, grabbing for the most parental love he or she can get.

As we grow older, though, we begin to need the love of brothers and sisters, too. The prodigal needed his father's love and forgiveness, to be sure, but he also needed his brother's love and acceptance.

Growing in Christ is growing in our willingness to share parental love and to express love to our brothers and sisters.

Lord, help me build bridges back to my brothers and sisters.

**Restoring family relationships often starts with a card, a letter, or a phone call.**

# ■ APPLE TREES

Matt. 7:15-20: "Thus, by their fruit you will recognize them" (v. 20).

When Marge and Arne Davidov bought their first house, they were glad to see a good-sized apple tree in the backyard. They moved in during January and didn't think much about the tree until spring when Marge noticed that the blossoms were not all the same color. When she pointed it out to Arne he said, "That's strange," and went on mowing the lawn.

Even in midsummer, when the little apples were developing, they noticed nothing. It wasn't until the fruit started to mature that Arne shouted, "That's a grafted tree." There were five varieties of apples.

They also noticed that former owners hadn't been too selective about pruning branches, so that two varieties of apples now dominated the whole tree.

Our lives are like that. There are many possibilities in us—good fruit, poor fruit, fruit fit for different purposes, perhaps even bitter fruit or fruit apt to rot or become wormy.

The Spirit can work in our lives to prune us toward the best and most productive fruits that are in us. We can let the Spirit do that; we can ask him to.

 Lord, make my life useful and worthwhile, and fruitful.

**Talking with friends and associates or a pastor can sometimes help us recognize whether our lives are becoming more or less fruitful.**

# ■ THE CIDER PRESS

Psalm 127: "Unless the Lord builds the house, its builders labor in vain" (v. 1).

One year Marge and Arne's apple tree was just loaded with fruit. Arne decided to build a cider press. He had seen presses at auctions and knew in principle how they worked. He busied himself all one Saturday fashioning a pegged box of oak slats and a frame into which he could slip the bumper jack from his car to supply the needed pressure.

When Marge called him for supper, he wasn't quite through. "Can you wait a bit?" She could. Arne put on the finishing touches, then eagerly poured a load of apples into the press and started the jack click-clicking down.

Marge knew when Arne came upstairs and slumped into his chair that it hadn't worked. "Six drops!" he said. "Six drops from a half bushel of apples."

A year later, long after the press was cut up for kindling, Arne read in an article that you also have to have an apple *shredder*. You can't press cider out of whole apples.

There are times when faith needs to work in concern with some other force—like Alcoholics Anonymous or a marriage counselor or simply a group of other people of faith. Maybe to handle a drinking problem or a marital problem, maybe to tackle a big project at church we need some help to feed the right stuff into the machinery of our faith.

 Lord, keep me from laboring in vain, from wasting my efforts and my faith by being too independent.

**Sometimes a bit of research helps. We can study up on our problems and our concerns—even learn more about faith itself.**

# ■ MY PARTNER IS AN ALCOHOLIC

Luke 21:34-36: "Be careful, or your hearts will be weighed down with dissipation, drunkenness, and the anxieties of life, and that day will close on you unexpectedly like a trap" (v. 34).

He's an alcoholic." The truth hit Sam Flax like a linebacker. "That's what all this nonsense has been about."

When Sam realized that his partner was an alcoholic, he suddenly could see the patterns clearly: all the times his partner had called in sick, all the times he had asked Sam to fill in at the last moment, all the times he had seemed vague and incoherent when Sam had called after supper to double-check appointments or ask questions.

Sam's first reaction was anger. "Why me?" he asked. "Why should I be so lucky as to have an alcoholic partner?" He thought not only of what he had been through with broken appointments and bad communications in the past six months, but he also thought of what he was going to have to go through before things got better. There would be treatments, maybe hospitalization. Sam was going to be saddled with the whole operation.

Sam's second reaction was pity—and love. "He's my friend, he's my partner, he needs help—and he needs it now." Sam picked up the phone and began dialing. He would call AA first.

Lord, make me sensitive to drug abuse. Protect me from it and make me more able to understand and help others.

**Before trying to help or understand those who abuse drugs, it is well to ask the specialists and to read and pray.**

# ■ THE JOB OFFER

1 Cor. 3:10-15: "If what he has built survives, he will receive his reward" (v. 14).

Giving up security is hard," Marshall said to his wife. He was staring at a contract and job description on the kitchen table in front of him.

"Could you take a leave of absence from CanTrol?"

"Not to take another job, I couldn't. That's like having your cake and eating it, too."

"Is it such an even balance between the two?" Paula asked.

"It is. JonCo is newer, more risky—but I could move up faster. CanTrol is safe. I've done good work there, and I could stay indefinitely."

"What does God say?"

"God isn't saying right now."

Marshall has prayed about his decision. He still isn't sure. What he and Paula will discover as they think and talk and pray in the next few days is that God doesn't promise us comfort and security, but God does promise to sustain us.

They will take the risk. They will talk about the risk of faith and how Jesus and his disciples lived day by day. They will talk about the early church living with fear and uncertainty and how the work went on even with changes in leadership. They will talk about how, above all else, they have their faith and they have each other. So what if JonCo did fold? So what?

Marshall took the job.

Lord, help us to face opportunities and challenges in faith. Help us to calculate our risks through faith and prayer.

**Risk and change are the spices of life; security is the meat and potatoes. Sometimes God helps us decide whether we are hungry or bored.**

# ■ BERRY TALE

Gen. 3:17-19: "It will produce thorns and thistles for you . . . " (v. 18).

If you hike in the Pacific Northwest in the summertime, you are likely to happen upon huge thickets of wild blackberries. If you are not familiar with them, you might taste a berry carefully, discover it to be delicious, and then pick a few more, remembering that you have seen thickets of such vines everywhere.

"Why don't the local people pick these?" you might ask yourself. At about the same time you reach in deep for that extra-juicy-looking berry and discover why. Thorns. Sharp and long and fish-hooked inward, these little rapiers would be perfect for a Mexican fighting cock.

The seasoned western berry lover goes out picking with a short ladder, boots, leather jacket, gauntlet welding gloves, and a tank helmet.

Some of life's enticements are like those juicy berries. They look pretty good until we discover the thorns—the tension and fatigue of overwork, the guilt and broken trust in an extramarital excursion, the hypertension and overweight from rich foods.

There are lots of wonderful berries in this world, but enjoying them safely and wisely requires awareness, preparedness, insight, self-control, and moderation. Otherwise we find ourselves in thorns.

 Lord, don't let me be either blinded or hooked by what looks like pleasure.

**Sometimes if we discuss choices and decisions with trusted friends we can avoid foolish mistakes.**

# ■ SAVINGS AND INVESTMENTS

Matt. 6:19-21, 24:  "For where your treasure is, there your heart will be also" (v. 21).

Elmer Ellefson reached retirement age wondering what he had to show for his life's work. What he often regretted were properties and belongings that he had let slip through his fingers over the years that would have been worth plenty if he had them now.

He thought of cars: Model Ts and Model As and a Star and even a Hupmobile. He thought of his uncle's lakeshore property up north that no one developed. It had seemed so worthless in the 1950s that the family had let it go for taxes. It was now a beautifully developed state park worth millions.

He thought of the little farm they almost had bought about the time Pearl Harbor was bombed and how, instead of settling down in that lovely spot, he had gone off to three and a half years in the marines and ended up with a bullet hole in his left shoulder. That little farm was now ritzy suburbia, 40 acres of fine homes on half-acre lots. What were those lots worth now?

But when Elmer remembered to thank God that he wasn't *killed* at Anzio, that Bess was still with him, and that they had raised a healthy and happy family, he didn't mind so much his lifetime investment record.

Lord, make me content with what I have instead of always wishing for what I haven't.

**Counting our blessings is one sure way of becoming more content. We should do it often.**

# ■ THE BIG CITY WILDERNESS

Matt. 4:1-11: "Then Jesus was led by the Spirit into the desert to be tempted by the devil" (v. 1).

Every time Andy Sherwin goes away from home on business, he can feel his moral immune system weaken. Out of his familiar surroundings, separated from his old and trusted support systems of home, family, neighbors, and church, he can almost feel the devil lurking, poised to attack him at some weak moment.

Jesus was tempted in the wilderness. Andy's wilderness is always the big city, the bright lights, the "nobody-knows-me-here" psychology of a business trip. Here temptation often strikes in enticing ways.

The prodigal son did his wild and willful thing away from home. He went to the far country and there he tried everything. But in the back of his mind he knew there was home, and love. He went home.

Jesus resisted temptation in the wilderness. The prodigal in the far country did not. It is far better to say no.

Notice what happened when Jesus said no: "Then the devil left him, and angels came and attended him." Andy Sherwin has felt that, too. When he has resisted, he has walked with angels. When he has weakened, he has, like the prodigal, known the forgiveness of his loving father.

 Lord, fill me with strength to resist temptation when I am away from home.

**On business trips and at conventions it helps to take along spiritual reminders of home: your Bible, your family's devotional booklet, and pictures of your family.**

# ■ WE'LL DO IT

John 14:15-18: "I will not leave you as orphans; I will come to you" (v. 18).

Phil Jarvis was an accountant; he was also fairly handy with tools. Phil's house had a section of leaky flat roof over the front staircase. After fighting leaks for a winter, Phil decided to tear off the flat roof and build a hip roof that would shed water.

He had never built a roof before, so he studied the inside of several attics and also consulted a few carpenter's books. He built the roof rafter by rafter, cutting and fitting each piece. He knew he was doing it the hard way, but he also knew he had done well when a carpenter neighbor shouted up at him, "You build a pretty good roof for a banker."

When the roof was almost finished, Phil got a call about teaching Sunday school. His first impulse was to say no. What he did say was, "I'll think about it."

"I'm no teacher," Phil thought. "Suppose I mess things up or teach the wrong things?" Then he thought, "I'm no carpenter either, but I've just built a roof—and all alone. Teaching, I guess I could have lots of help—especially from the best teacher of all."

Phil called back ready to say, "I'll do it." What he did say was, "*We'll* do it."

 Lord, remind me every day that I am not alone. Make your presence felt, especially when I serve your church.

**Volunteering on self-confidence alone can undermine our confidence in God's providence and help.**

## ■ FISHERMEN FOR GOD

Mark 1:16-20: "Come, follow me . . . and I will
make you fishers of men" (v. 17).

On an autumn businessmen's retreat, Arlie Kivens
watched some fishermen tending gill nets in the river
across from their camp. He thought of Jesus' disciples,
Peter and Andrew and James and John, who were also
commercial fishermen. "They used nets, too," he
thought.

When Jesus called Peter and the others to be
disciples, he said he would make them fishers of men.
He taught them, however, as he teaches us, that
fishing for men is more like angling than like gill
netting. In a gill net a fish hasn't a chance. It puts its
head through a hole too small for its body, then
realizing that it is caught, the fish swims even further
ahead and is fully trapped. There is no escape.

God doesn't use nets. God angles for us one by one
with words and with invitations and with love. God's
lures have neither hooks nor barbs. We are never
trapped. We are caught because we let God catch us.
And when God catches us, God doesn't eat us. God
feeds us.

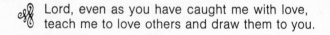 Lord, even as you have caught me with love,
teach me to love others and draw them to you.

**Tomorrow I will speak to Bill about Jesus—but with
the gentleness of a dry fly on quiet water.**

# ■ SQUIRRELS

Rom. 6:5-11: "If we have been united with him in his death, we will certainly also be united with him in his resurrection" (v. 5).

One bright and early spring day nine squirrels played in David Norton's backyard trees. He figured it was their first or second day out of hibernation. Many winters his backyard squirrels didn't hibernate at all. Those winters they would come every day to eat the corn and bread crusts he put out for them. This had been a particularly tough winter, though. The squirrels had hibernated for over a month.

Dave had never seen so many squirrels at once, and he had never seen them so wild. They ran over every aerial route, chased each other across the snow, round and round the tree trunks, up and down limbs, leaping over great spaces, and climbing all over the stucco sides of his house.

Dave admitted that he didn't know how a squirrel thinks, but decided that if he were a squirrel just out of hibernation, he would be awfully happy to be alive after such a long sleep. He'd run wild, too, wild and free and thankful. He'd run with abandon and with joy; he'd run with his friends and he'd run alone. He'd run and run and run.

Dave wondered if it might be like that for us on the first day of the resurrection.

 Keep the vision of our forever ever before us, Lord, so that we can better live our now.

**There is much more to life than waiting for eternity. We need to live our joy, our hope, and our love.**

# ■ MY BOSS IS LIKE KING HEROD

Matt. 2:7-16:  "And having been warned in a dream
not to go back to Herod, they returned to their
country by another route"  (v. 12).

Andrew Lee sat down one Saturday evening with a
Bible and commentaries to prepare a Sunday school
lesson on King Herod. After reading for 20 minutes
he yelled, "Hey, Jenny. Herod is just like my boss."

King Herod was indeed a jealous, psychotic
monomaniac. Obsessed with protecting his rule, he
even killed two of his own sons to guard his throne.
His attempt to kill Jesus by killing all the two-year-
old boys around Bethlehem was predictable.

God told the Wise Men and Mary and Joseph to
stay away from Herod. With a leader that bad and
with a baby who had already been called a "prince
of peace," what else could they do?

The world still has too many Herods, and many
people like Andrew Lee work for them or, even worse,
are governed by them. Andrew can do as the Wise
Men and the holy family did. He can find another job
and leave his boss behind. Most people of the world
aren't that lucky.

As Christians we want to know about and care
about oppressed people and their inhuman leaders.
We can work for and vote for and pray for good
leadership in our own country and around the world.

 Lord, help me to recognize good leaders and
support them. Help all oppressed people win
new leadership and new freedoms.

This week I will ask my pastor what our church is
doing and what I can do for oppressed people in the
world.

# ■ THE BLESSING OF TOUGH TIMES

Luke 13:22-30: "Make every effort to enter through the narrow door, because many, I tell you, will try to enter and will not be able to" (v. 24).

After the recession of the early 1980s, experts predicted that we consumers would never return to our wasteful, spendthrift ways. Even after short money, unemployment, and conservation drove gas prices down to half of what they'd been during the crisis '70s, experts weren't predicting a return to large, heavy automobiles. People on our continent apparently have learned a lesson.

There is some advantage to hardship, shortage, and privation. Even in the church we learn in hard times to care for resources and care for each other. By contrast, in the affluent '50s our churches were full, money was plentiful, and congregations were building large, plush sanctuaries. Air was conditioned, pews were padded, the Christian message and Christians themselves were softened until like ice cream on a warm day they nearly melted away. Thank God we can look forward in the '80s to a church with tougher members who have been through tighter times.

When Jesus said "enter through the narrow door" he was warning us that Christianity is not comfortable and easy answers, but disturbance, struggle, and work.

 Lord, strengthen me for the everyday challenges and struggles of following Jesus.

My church membership has been too easy. I'll go to the phone right now and volunteer to serve or teach or help.

# ■ RIGHT IN STYLE

Matt. 3:1-10: "John's clothes were made of camel's hair, and he had a leather belt around his waist. His food was locusts and wild honey" (v. 4).

When Mickey put on his John the Baptist costume for the church play, his father broke out laughing. "You look just like some of those street people I saw in L.A. last week," he said.

Even as they laughed together, Mickey's dad thought about styles of dress and styles of people and even styles of Christianity. He thought of TV preachers who wear business suits, of the pope who wears many layers of the finest vestments, and of his own preacher, who is somewhere in between.

John the Baptist and Jesus were men of very different styles. John's austere clothing and his austere diet were signs of his austere message: "You brood of vipers!" he said. "Produce fruit in keeping with repentance." John was beheaded for his tough honesty, his stubborn fearlessness.

Jesus wore the ordinary cloak and sandals of the day. His style was often gentle. He healed people by laying hands on them. He loved children. He would associate with anyone, even tax collectors and prostitutes. His message was love for God and love for each other. Jesus was crucified for his love and submission.

The Spirit speaks to us in many ways, with many voices, from many sources. We test the message to see if it is of God, being careful not to be put off by style alone.

 God — Father, Son, and Spirit — help me to hear your voice no matter who is shouting or whispering or writing it.

**This summer I will take my family to other churches so they can see and we can talk about different styles and different approaches to the good news of Jesus.**

46

# THE CURE FOR DEATH

Matt. 4:23-25: "People brought to him all who were ill with various diseases, those suffering severe pain, the demon-possessed, the epileptics and the paralytics, and he healed them" (v. 24).

Bob Ethelridge knew he had no business on the same wrestling mat with Coach Wilson, but he had volunteered to help coach and he wanted to do his best. Bob was a 38-year-old English teacher, but the boys didn't seem to mind.

One day when Bob and Coach Wilson were demonstrating how to bridge out of a pin hold, Bob's hernia popped. Two weeks later he was in the hospital awaiting surgery. He was home a few days later, and in several weeks was back to normal activity.

Our modern health care is amazing. Ancient medicine was not so exacting. Early patients were bled, purged, starved, fed strange herbs, and smeared with weird remedies. Surgery was either crude sutures or even cruder amputation. No wonder Jesus the healer drew such crowds.

But Jesus didn't fix just earthly ills. He knew, as we all know, that even after a life of excellent health and even having available the best health care, the end of life, the end of health is death.

For death Jesus alone has the cure.

 Lord Jesus, cure the curse of death in me. Make me more alive both now and forever.

**Think back to when you were sick or hospitalized. Were you lonely, apprehensive, or afraid? You could share those feelings with friends who are fighting illness or facing surgery.**

# ■ EELPOUT

Mark 2:13-17: "Why does he eat with tax collectors and 'sinners'?" (v. 16).

When Warren Madden learned that Grandpa Olsen was going to set nets under the ice for whitefish he asked to go along. Once the nets were in place, they tended them every two days. They caught plenty of nice whitefish, but once in a while they would pull up an eelpout or "ling" as Grandpa Olsen used to call them.

Warren thought eelpout were the ugliest fish he had ever seen. They had spotted, slimy skins, brown catfish heads, puffy gray bellies, and snakelike tails. The large ones also had protruding jaw hinges that would twist into and ruin the fine nylon nets. Most ice fishermen hated them. They'd cut them out of the nets and throw them as far as they could out on the ice to freeze.

Warren asked the college biologist about eelpout and learned that it was a freshwater codfish and one of the best eating fish in the northern lakes. He kept eelpout after that and enjoyed some fine fried fillets and chowders.

Many a sinner looks like an eelpout on the outside— too riddled with sin, too sick, too ugly, too far gone. Jesus got pretty chummy with a few eelpout in his time: the tax collectors, prostitutes, outcasts, and lepers. He could see the tender flesh inside, savory and good. Some of his best friends and favorite people were eelpout.

 Lord, help me see the possibilities for good in all people.

**Maybe this week I can take a new look at some of the people around me.**

# ■ FOUNDATIONS

Matt. 7:24-27:   "Everyone who hears these words of mine and puts them into practice is like a wise man who built his house on the rock" (v. 24).

Geologist Clarence Fossum and his wife Carla moved from Berkeley to Tulsa to Calgary to Houston in less than five years. What Clarence noticed about their several houses was the difference in foundations. It seemed to him that the more severe the climate, the better and more solid the foundations had to be.

Clarence decided it made economic sense for builders to use cement slabs in California, pylons on the Gulf Coast, and the even more expensive footing and full-basement construction for homes in the below-zero northern climates.

But as he read the passage about building on a rock in Matthew 7, Clarence wondered if people could also fit their foundations to their needs. He decided it was risky.

We can't even predict beforehand the storms we will have to weather. Those who think they have enough faith or religion and guess wrong are blown away or drowned.

Jesus' parable tells us to build our spiritual footings to weather the worst. Onslaughts by the world, political and economic upheaval, accident, sickness, and death sometimes make extreme demands on our spiritual resources. It is well then to have our footings deep.

 Lord Jesus, make my faith more solid, my strength more sure.

**Regular study of the Bible deepens the foundations of faith.**

## ■ FEELING WORTHLESS

Job 5:17-26:  "He wounds, but he also binds up; he injures, but his hands also heal" (v. 18).

Alvin's proposal was rejected. He really believed in it; he thought the agency would go with his proposal. They rejected it, and he felt worthless.

Al couldn't help thinking about the book of Job. He opened his Bible to it that evening. Job had everything; then he lost everything. But through it all, and above all, Job kept his faith.

Al was moved by the laments of Job. He was sorry he himself had no wife with whom to share his rejection, but he was glad he didn't have a snarling witch like Job's wife—nor friends like his either.

Al reflected on what the proposal had cost him: a little over a month's work, and some expenses, too—travel, phone calls, graphics for his presentation. Too bad the agency hadn't gone for it. But he had learned a lot. There were some sound ideas in that folder. He would take another look at it.

Job had faith; so did Al. Faith in God meant knowing he was a loved person even when he felt rejected. Al would try again, and again, and again if necessary, even if it took the faith of Job.

 Lord, help me to climb over setbacks and to grow in adversity. Make my faith in you build faith in myself.

**Looking back we see that God has allowed some doors to close on us so that we might see others opening.**

# ■ THE CHRISTIAN SALT PILL

Matt. 5:1-13: "You are the salt of the earth. But if the salt has lost its saltiness, how can it be made salty again?" (v. 13).

Orville laughs now when he tells about that embarrassing day in 1944 when he ate the salt pill. He was in seventh grade. His father was a naval officer in Florida and the whole family went one Sunday to services at base chapel and then to the officers' mess for dinner. As they stood in line Orville noticed a dispenser of pills above the water fountain. "What are those?" he asked.

"Salt pills," his dad said. "When the men sweat a lot they take a pill to replace the salt."

When no one was looking Orville took a salt pill. Five minutes later, just after he had gotten his tray filled with fried chicken and mashed potatoes and gravy—everything he liked—he threw up all over it.

Salt is powerful stuff. Too little will give us heat prostration and too much will make us sick. Even normal amounts will aggravate high blood pressure and cardiac problems.

Jesus said to his followers, "You are the salt of the earth." Maybe he meant that if we force ourselves on others, we can be hard to stomach. He certainly meant that we Christians give flavor to society, that we fill a great need.

 Lord, give me a proper sense of witness. Help me offer just the right amount of salt to those who need it.

**You might ask your friends at church or your pastor about your own saltiness.**

# ■ PATIENCE AND IMPATIENCE

James 5:7-11: "You too, be patient and stand firm, because the Lord's coming is near" (v. 8).

When Jim Clifford's dog Betsy went into heat, he kept her in the garage. For exercise he chained her to the clothes pole and sat guard on the upstairs porch with a BB gun. A dozen dogs came and went, responding predictably to the sting of a pellet, but one bushy shepherd type shrugged off his shots, moved just out of range, and bided his time. Then the phone rang. Several weeks later it was obvious that Jim had been distracted.

Jim's whole family waited impatiently for Betsy's time, especially Jim's son, Steve. One Saturday afternoon when Steve's Cub Scout pack was meeting at their house, Betsy came padding home, proudly carrying her first pup in her mouth.

Jim hustled her into the newspaper nest they had prepared in the garage. Then he hollered for the Cub Scouts, and they all sat around on cement blocks, hands on knees, watching and waiting to midwife. The pups came at unpredictable times and came quickly. Most of the time the boys were outside shooting baskets. No boy saw more than half of the deliveries, and Steve missed them all—all nine.

Jim decided that patience is an adult virtue. Impatience undoubtedly moves us toward important human achievements, but patience often grants us access to the slow and quiet miracles of life.

 Lord, give me patience to wait for beauty, truth, and growth. Enrich my life with your gradual miracles.

**Cultivating patience makes us better parents—and husbands, too.**

# ■ TROUBLED WATERS

Rom. 15:7-13: "May the God of hope fill you with all joy and peace as you trust in him, so that you may overflow with hope by the power of the Holy Spirit" (v. 13).

At the point where a river meets the ocean, water can be flowing either way. When the tide is coming in, water may actually be moving upstream, causing fierce turbulence.

Brian and Shelley Davidson learned that frightening truth one summer on the Umpqua River in Oregon. They foolishly motored their small fishing boat out onto a calm ocean. Later in the afternoon, when they turned back toward the mouth of the river, the tide had turned.

Twice they tried to motor through the churning water but turned back. The third time, as Brian was giving his 15-horse engine everything it had, a Coast Guard cutter pulled up and stood by, ready to come to their aid. On this attempt Brian's and Shelley's small boat made it through the churning waters. Even though they had not needed the cutter's help, the purr and hum of its engines and the smiling seamen with ring buoys in their hands had given them extra hope and confidence to make it through.

Much of life is like those churning tidewaters. Fighting them alone is foolish. The Spirit's presence can empower us to cruise through almost any turbulence.

 Holy Spirit, guide my ways through troubled waters. Help me to know you are there in the most frightening of times.

**Pray for the Spirit's presence and help. The Spirit will make you a more determined and bolder follower of Jesus.**

## ■ UNEMPLOYED

Luke 12:22-31: "And do not set your heart on what you will eat or drink; do not worry about it" (v. 29).

Warren Ripley was unemployed. He couldn't remember a time when he hadn't worked — from the summer after ninth grade through four years after high school through his two-year hitch in the Air Force and on and on for the last eight years.

Warren knew he was a good employee. He had never had trouble with any supervisor — not bosses, not foremen, not even that surly drill sergeant in training camp. Warren worked hard, did his job, and caused no one any unnecessary trouble.

But this was different. The company was bankrupt. His job had ended yesterday, and it wasn't his fault. "They never lost a penny on me," he told Anna. "I didn't run them into bankruptcy."

He wondered what he would do. Jobs were scarce, very scarce. He could draw unemployment, and Anna was working, but without his paycheck they would soon lose the house.

Warren and Anna talked and prayed and talked some more for that whole weekend. They decided that God would provide for them somehow. Warren would begin job hunting Monday — and he would do it confidently.

 Lord, make me aware of your care, certain of your providence, no matter what.

**God provides for us in so many ways—in abilities, in opportunities, in achievements.**

# ■ EVEN ON A FOOL'S ERRAND

Eccles. 4:9-12: "Pity the man who falls and has no one to help him up" (v. 10).

Bert and Evan tried to swim out to Round Lake Island. They had a canoe hidden in the bushes on the island, and they needed it the next morning for a race. Only teenagers would try anything so foolish, swimming halfway across a lake by July's full moon.

They hadn't gone far when Evan knew he wasn't going to make it. He sputtered to Bert, "I'm already tired, and we aren't even halfway."

Bert was a strong swimmer and pushed Evan ahead of him with the tired swimmer's carry, then let him swim some more, then helped him again. Together in that off-and-on way they made it to the island.

Trusting in the Lord is like having a strong swimmer constantly at our side. When we are tired, he encourages us. When we are desperate, he lets us ride on his power. When we are on fool's journeys, he will usually help us back to shore for a new start. But when the challenge is worthwhile, he will help us carry on, to finish and reach our goals.

Lord, encourage me with your truth, carry me with your strength.

It is important first to set sensible goals, then to trust in the Lord to help us reach them.

# ■ TO GO AGAINST CONSCIENCE

2 Cor. 1:12: "Now this is our boast: Our conscience testifies that we have conducted ourselves in the world . . . in the holiness and sincerity that are from God."

Harry Kane sat on his rolling stool staring at the brake mechanism. "I can't do it," he said, shaking his head. "That new shop foreman must have horns and a tail. He's got me talking to myself."

The new foreman had only been at Gundy Motors for three weeks, and this was the fourth job Harry had been asked to do that he didn't believe in.

"I can't put new linings in these scored-up things," he said, running his fingers over the rutted brake drums. He knew it wouldn't take more than a half hour extra to resurface them. "A lousy $18 shop time," he thought. "He has two standards," Harry muttered. "He does extra work on customers' cars and not half enough on our used cars — just enough to get them sold."

"I can't do it that way," he mumbled, and carried the two drums over to the drum lathe. As he clamped the first drum in the machine he said to himself, "I've worked here 17 years. Just let him try to fire me. Right is right and wrong is wrong. I'm going to do these brakes right." Harry began to hum a hymn to the rhythmic ringing of the lathe.

 Lord, school my conscience to see and know what is right. Then give me courage to do it.

Examine some of the work you are asked to do day after day. Is it always the best? Is it always right? What could you yourself do to improve matters?

# ■ ANSWER TO PRAYER

Matt. 8:1-4: "Lord, if you are willing, you can make me clean" (v. 2).

Those words were a leper's leap of faith. He believed that if Jesus was willing he could heal the leprosy. Jesus was willing. The man was healed.

Not all prayers are answered in such an obvious way. Sam prays, "Lord Jesus, if you are willing, my baby will not die." Carl prays, "Lord Jesus, if you are willing, my daughter will get off of drugs." Leroy prays, "Lord Jesus, if you are willing, my business won't go bankrupt."

What if Jesus doesn't? Should they then see God as cruel, uncaring, remote from their deepest needs?

Faithful and earnest prayers are always answered, but sometimes in unexpected ways. Sam's child who dies may have been spared a catastrophe that only God could foresee. Carl's heartwrenching struggle with his troubled teenager may deepen their family understanding and love and faith. Leroy's bankruptcy can give him a new vision, new direction, and new goals.

It takes great faith to interpret answers to prayer. For most of us it takes time. Matt Borland remembers being depressed about a job he had prayed for but didn't get. Several years later he knew for sure that getting that job would have been a big mistake. God answered his prayer by protecting him from the wrong work at the wrong time in the wrong place.

 Lord Jesus, deepen my faith and understanding. Show me your real will in difficult times.

**Look back and list some of the times God has said no to you and see if you may not be as well or better off because of it.**

# ■ THE OBNOXIOUS ASSISTANT

Matt. 13:24-30: " 'Sir, didn't you sow good seed in your field? Where then did the weeds come from?' 'An enemy did this,' he replied" (vv. 27-28).

I can't stand that guy," Paul said. Martha listened patiently. "He taking over my team. And he doesn't know diddly about the game." Paul had never been so upset about a volunteer job before. Martha could see this was different. This new assistant coach had him buffaloed.

"Have you prayed about it?" she asked.

"You bet I have. And I've reminded myself of what Jesus said about loving your enemies."

"Is he really an enemy? Is it that bad?"

"Well, after two weeks of practice he has contradicted me a half dozen times, he has several times suggested intimidation as a strategy of play, and he constantly swears in front of the boys."

"Don't you think he'll cut his own throat with that approach?"

"Sure he will. But what happens to the team in the meantime?"

Paul's dilemma was not an easy one. He was caught between concern for his team, disgust with a misguided colleague, and the need to examine his own motives. Paul had to weigh patience against confrontation. He had to measure his frustration against what was good for his team, putting all options under the microscope of Christ's love.

 Lord, help me in any decision to see all sides of the issue — and then to see your will in my choice of action.

**If you, like Paul, have to deal with difficult colleagues, discuss and weigh each of the options with caution, humility, and prayer. Never shoot from the hip with volatile relationships.**

## ■ BLUEBONNETS

Luke 12:22-31: "Not even Solomon in all his splendor was arrayed like one of these" (v. 27).

Bluebonnet Day was the greatest. The picnic was superb because Garfield Kiel had planned it. The long drive was tolerable, even enjoyable, because he sensed which couples would ride together best. And the Texas wild flowers were at their peak. The car caravan stopped again and again to gaze over those seas of flowers in field after field. Blue, white, pink, purple — but mostly white. No picking. Against the law. Just look. Feast.

They drove back into town at dusk, aware that they had shared a miracle. Garfield Kiel had given them that gift, and a gift of acceptance too, in a place where Yankees weren't always too welcome.

Jesus did that a lot. He took people who were out of place, out of luck, out of favor. He took people who couldn't see beauty or who didn't know where beauty was, and he showed them. He put them together with other people. He fed them in every way. He showed them life. He gave them life. With Jesus, bluebonnets are always in season — everywhere.

 Lord, help me to see beauty and to share it.

**There are beauty spots around my town too. I should share them with. . . .**

# ■ JOB SECURITY

Prov. 12:8-14: ". . . the work of his hands rewards him" (v. 14).

Times were tough. The economy had turned down, and Lee Ingram kept a worried eye on his paycheck. He knew that some employees in his area were sure to be laid off, and he was determined *not* to be one of them.

Lee decided to become the model employee. His plan was to quit being the monkeywrench he had been. He had always been the one to make the suggestions and to deliver the collective complaints of his assembly team. If the quotas were too high, Lee complained. When one supervisor constantly harassed young Cathy, Lee came to her defense and the supervisor was fired.

But now Lee was scared. He spent two months trying hard not to make waves. Then the production manager called him in. "What's wrong, Lee?" he asked. After much discussion Lee admitted that he was afraid of losing his job.

"The only way you'll lose your job here is if you keep on playing mouse in the corner. We need your suggestions and complaints. I can practically promise you job security if you'll go out there and be your old snarling self again."

Lee smiled as he walked out. "They'd better not try to fire any of my team either," he thought.

 Lord, teach me to be myself, always.

**Playing a part, being other than ourselves, finally catches up to us.**

# ■ THE PRETTY GOOD SAMARITAN

Luke 10:29-37:   "And who is my neighbor?" (v. 29).

Good Samaritans have always been a bit rare, but
we all know some "pretty good" Samaritans. John
Manson tells of the summer he returned home from a
year of study on the West Coast. He and his wife
and two toddlers had an uneventful trip pulling their
U-Haul until they began climbing the Bighorn
Mountains in a roiling thunderstorm. Slowly they
made their ascent.

As they crossed the deserted plateau in the flash
and crash of the storm, John worried about the load,
the brakes, and the hairpin curve descent ahead.
They talked of sleeping in the car, but it was too
lonely up there.

Just then a pickup passed them and stopped in the
middle of the deserted road ahead. Now what?
Robbery, murder? A rancher got out and walked back
to their car. "I'll take ya'll down," he said. "Just watch
my brakelights." John and Eva followed him for 45
minutes down the Bighorn's eastern face. At the
bottom he opened his window, waved, and scooted
north to Montana.

Thank God for "pretty good" Samaritans who will
stop to help a stranger. We will see them often—
and we will also be them.

 Lord, teach me to give and receive help with
understanding, with grace, and with love.

**List some of the "pretty good" Samaritans you have
known as a way of asking how helpful you are to
others.**

# ■ PROTECTIVE FATHERING

Gen. 22:1-14:  " 'The fire and wood are here,'
Isaac said, 'but where is the lamb for the burnt
offering?' "  (v. 7).

Don Roth's heart nearly stopped when he saw what
his son was doing. Don had been so busy admiring
the turquoise beauty of Crater Lake that he hadn't
noticed his three-year-old climb over the stone wall
and begin chasing chipmunks on the grassy ledge that
abruptly became a 100-foot sheer cliff.

Every father wants to protect his children from
such dangers—and from hurts, too, both physical and
mental. Every father hurts when his son breaks a bone
or gets skinned up or is delirious with fever. Every
father aches when his daughter is ignored by the
neighbor kids or is jilted by a boy or doesn't make
the team. We hurt for our kids and want for them
health and safety and acceptance and joy.

How well we understand Abraham and ache with
him, shuddering even as we read how he raised the
knife over his child of promise.

But God was only testing Abraham. God is also a
father and aches with us. For God there was no
snatching the boy back over the wall like Don Roth
did, no last-second reprieve as with Abraham and
Isaac. God watched his Son die. He understands.

 Lord, teach us by your love to be more caring,
more loving fathers. Forgive our failures,
through your Son who died.

**Maybe today we should tell our sons—and our
daughters, too—how much their health and safety
mean to us.**

# ■ BREAD WITHOUT SWEAT

Matt. 4:1-4: "If you are the Son of God, tell these stones to become bread" (v. 3).

Isn't it just like the devil to tell us that work is the problem. When we read how humankind lost Eden, we get the idea that the curse was work.

The curse wasn't work, of course. The curse was sin. If sinful humankind had stayed in a no-work Eden, who knows what might have happened.

Work wasn't Adam's curse; it was his blessing. Adam and Eve and all of us are blessed by work. By work we grow back into the image of God. By work we explore our strengths and weaknesses, our gifts and our possibilities. By work we learn to be together and build together and endure and even enjoy this pilgrimage, this midway island on our journey to eternity.

By the Sea of Galilee Jesus gave 5000 and more people bread and fish with no work. For that free lunch they wanted to make him king. He refused to be a king of daily bread in order that he could become the bread of eternal life.

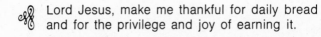 Lord Jesus, make me thankful for daily bread and for the privilege and joy of earning it.

**Even as we buy and use food carefully and conserve it, we can be learning how we can help feed the world's starving.**

## ■ FIRST IMPRESSIONS

Prov. 20:20-30:   "The glory of young men is their
strength, gray hair the splendor of the old" (v. 29).

Allan Hirsch grew a beard in graduate school. It
was brown and wiry and beautiful. "Makes you look
good," his wife said.

Just before Christmas, 18 years later, Allan saw a
picture of himself with that beard. He *did* look good
—strong, virile. He started to grow another, but this
time it came out more than half gray. Somehow that
wasn't the same.

Allan kept the beard until Ash Wednesday – about
15 weeks – then shaved it off. His wife was furious.
She loved the beard. "Makes you look distinguished,"
she said. "More mature," she said.

He did look more mature – *about 20 years more
mature.*

Their church was taking pictures for the new
congregational directory just before Allan shaved.
He was pictured in the directory with his beard.
There he stood beside his wife, looking like her
father. "Who is that old man?" their friends teased
when the directory came out.

How often we see or evaluate people in just one
fragment, one moment of their lives, a blink of the
camera's eye. Are they really themselves in that
moment? Is that the way they always are?

We can be thankful that God doesn't judge us on
moments – good moments or bad – especially in that
unpredictable moment of our death.

Help me, Lord, to take more time, to be more
careful in my evaluation of others.

**Getting to know people better often removes first
impression prejudices.**

# ■ THE OLYMPIC CHRISTIAN

Matt. 11:16-19: "To what can I compare this generation? They are like children sitting in the marketplaces and calling out to others, 'We played the flute for you, and you did not dance; we sang a dirge, and you did not mourn' " (vv. 16-17).

When a player finds just the right game or hobby, he throws himself into it with abandon, with energy, and with love. It thrills him, fulfills him, distills him into something stronger, wiser, swifter, more energetic, and even more daring.

Jesus and John the Baptist were showing people of their time different sides of the same game. John played by strict and harsh rules: fasting, austerity, extreme self-control. Jesus' game seemed to have no rules at all, a kind of free running, wide-sweeping business. In some towns where Jesus and John had both preached and healed and worked, it seemed that no one wanted to play either way. The game was engaging, extremely important, deadly, and eternal— but no one wanted to play.

Christianity comes to us in many guises, with many guidelines and many variations. A man who doesn't explore many of them may be missing that ideal and special way of worship or life into which he might really throw himself.

 Lord Jesus, help me to keep seeking until I learn how to play this game of life your way.

**If I poured my golf enthusiasm, my handball energy, and my jogging endurance into Sunday morning worship, could I be an Olympic Christian?**

# ■ THE BOREDOM OF ROUTINE

Gal. 6:1-10: "Let us not become weary in doing good . . ." (v. 9).

Matt Lehrer sat at his desk grading his 14th set of lab reports for the term. He had been teaching for 26 years. How many lab reports would that be? He calculated: 16 per term makes 32 per year, or about 100 every three years. For 26 years that's about 850 sets. Average class size, 24. That's 24 x 850 or 12 x 1700 or 6 x 3400 — roughly 10,000 x 2. "I've graded 20,000 lab reports. Wow." Matt Lehrer decided he was bored.

He thought back to his college years and about his early interest in biological field work. During college he had spent his favorite summer of all time studying tidewater shellfish in Florida. "But what if I had stayed there?" he thought. "I never would have met Becky, and we wouldn't have had Cindy and John, and I wouldn't have had all those students who wrote all those reports. How many students were there? 24 a term —that's almost 50 a year — 1,300 in 26 years in biology alone. Add to that general science and math. I've had five or six thousand students over the years."

Matt Lehrer put his head in his hands and prayed a prayer of thanks: "Thank you, Lord, for Becky and the kids, and for the thousands of other folks' kids I have taught. Thanks for the blessed boredom that has made all this possible."

 Thank you, Lord, for the routine of work, for the comfort of knowing that some of my chores don't change.

**When routine drags and grates, try changing something else—your recreation, study, or prayer habits, for instance.**

# ■ SERVE HIM AS WE ARE

Luke 2:22-32: "It had been revealed to him by the Holy Spirit that he would not die before he had seen the Lord's Christ" (v. 26).

Three hundred students watched as Old Pastor John, age 99, the oldest retired clergyman in the state, capped off the campus Christmas party by holding up a faculty member's new baby and speaking from memory the Song of Simeon. The oldest man in town held the youngest man in town over his head and prayed, "Lord, now lettest thou thy servant depart in peace."

Simeon may have spent many years waiting for Jesus at the temple in Jerusalem. He was a man of great patience. His patience was rewarded.

Contrast Simeon with the fiery-eyed John the Baptist, probably the most impatient of all biblical characters. John preached and prepared for Jesus' coming for only a short time.

Both of these men achieved spiritual satisfaction and fulfillment by following the paths God had laid out for them. John died a martyr's violent death; Simeon probably died in bed. But both lives had counted. Both patience and impatience have their place. God can use all kinds.

We mistake what God expects if we try to rebuild ourselves on some other model, in some other mold. God may ask us to change our ways but never our natures. We are made in God's image. We can serve God as we are, with what we have.

🎵 Holy Spirit, help me also to see Christ and in him find peace.

**This week take an inventory of your own characteristics and capabilities to see how God has used them—or could use them.**

# ■ LUST IN THE OFFICE

2 Sam. 11:2-6: ". . . he saw from the roof a
woman bathing, and the woman was very beautiful"
(v. 2).

Ray Worthing was attracted to Alyce from the first
day she walked into the office. She started as
temporary help from the secretarial pool and her stay
became permanent. Ray watched her arranging her
things on the desk that first day and thought she
moved like an actress. He thought she was beautiful.

At home things were in a bit of a crisis for Ray. His
daughter was having some trouble in junior high, and
Ray and his wife were disagreeing, often arguing,
about how to handle her. The stress had cooled their
relationship. Ray had even stopped going to church
with his wife.

Just at this point Alyce appeared in the office. Ray,
frustrated and disturbed by the situation at home,
began to watch Alyce more and more. He even moved
his desk a foot or so to get a better view of her at the
typewriter.

Then Ray caught himself daydreaming of Alyce and
himself. "Lust," he said. "One of the deadly sins. Lust."
He could scarcely believe what he was thinking. He
knew of a few office romances, and on that day he
knew how they started to happen.

Before he left the office that day, Ray Worthing
called his pastor: "Pastor Bob? Carla and I are having
some trouble, and I'd like to talk to you about it."

 Lord, help me distinguish between admiration,
friendship, and lust. Protect me from sins of
mind and body.

**Talking to the pastor or a counselor can sometimes
clear the air and help restore relationships.**

# ■ IMPORTANT PEOPLE

Matt. 11:7-11: "I tell you the truth: Among those born of woman there has not risen anyone greater than John the Baptist; yet he who is least in the kingdom of heaven is greater than he" (v. 11).

Jack Griffin is an autograph hound. On his den wall he has pictures and signatures of movie stars, professional athletes, a president, three senators, seven congressmen, and five governors. Not one of them knows Jack Griffin by name.

Jesus knew quite a few wealthy and important people—Joseph of Arimathea and others. Toward the end of his life he met just about all the big shots in his area: Pilate, Herod, Caiaphas, and the whole Sanhedrin, the high council of the temple.

Even though he would meet all these powerful people, Jesus still named his cousin John as the greatest man who ever lived—and close seconds were his special friends—Peter, James, John, Matthew, and the others.

An autograph collector back then wouldn't have bothered with such people: a shaggy and primitive prophet who lived and preached in the Judean wilderness, a couple of fishermen, a tax collector, and a kid. But they were Jesus' special people and have become household names the world over. What made these ordinary people so important? Knowing Jesus.

That is still true. The devout Christian still makes the best of friends, the best of husbands or wives, the best of bosses, the best of employees.

Lord, give me eyes to see that all people are important.

**On those days when you think you're a nobody, make a list of all the people who know you by name. Start that list with God.**

# ■ MY BODY IS SHOT

1 Cor. 9:24-27: "I beat my body and make it my slave . . ." (v. 27).

Roger Moss stepped off the scale and exhaled audibly, shaking his head. "I've broken 200," he said. It was no record to be proud of.

The thankful side of his 200 pounds was that he felt blessed to have lived in a nation so filled with good things. If the Israelites could have chosen between the milk and honey of Jordan and the corn and wheat of Iowa and Illinois, Roger thought, he knew for sure how they would have chosen.

Roger had lived the good life for 45 years. For the first 40 it hadn't affected him much. He rode along on his natural good health and his average amounts of exercise. In the last five years, though, he had gained over 20 pounds and practically had given up exercise altogether. He didn't look good, and he didn't feel good, and he didn't like it.

Lately Roger has been thinking of his body as a temple, as the Bible says. He has decided to exercise more, eat less, and see if he can stem the tide of weight gain. He has decided that he could be a more energetic and useful steward and servant if he put himself back into good condition.

 Lord, help me to see my body as a temple and to worship you with it.

The best weight-loss program is a better selection of foods chosen for a gradual reduction in calories, and a gradual increase in exercise. This kind of control and maintenance is for life.

# ■ SPREADING THE NEWS

Matt. 9:27-30: "Jesus warned them sternly, 'See that no one knows about this.' But they went out and spread the news about him over that region" (v. 30).

Well, what would we expect? Who could keep still if some traveling preacher had healed his blindness— or even fixed his sprained thumb or cured a common cold? Healing is not something we keep still about. That Jesus could heal was the worst-kept secret in Galilee. Everyone he ever told to keep quiet about it blabbed the truth all over the place. That's why the large crowds soon became huge.

And this time there were two blind men. One man's story must have reinforced the other; one testimony must have built upon the other: "He was blind, and so was I. Now we *both* can see."

Jesus may not have healed our eyes or our ears or our limbs, but he has healed our hearts. We have been healed from a midnight more black than blindness; we have been healed of a crippling handicap more debilitating than amputation. Jesus has cured our leprosy of soul.

How can we keep that a secret? How can we go about the neighborhood, the shop, the plant, the office without mentioning that sometimes? We too have been cured. We have been fixed right at last. We too have good news. No one has ever told us not to tell either.

Lord, make me so thankful for the healing of Jesus that I can't help telling about it.

**Witnessing can begin in very small ways: whistling hymns, hanging a cross on a keychain, leaving a book like this one lying around for someone to browse through.**

# ■ PRESSURE AND STRESS

Matt. 9:14-17: "They pour new wine into new wineskins, and both are preserved" (v. 17).

What made old wineskins explode? Probably the carbon dioxide pressure against the stiffness and brittleness of weathered leather. Herman Sanford thought of Jesus' parable when he blew six bottles of his homemade root beer. He had bottled it in thin-glass, nonreturnable bottles that couldn't stand the pressure.

Daniel Hershey had the opposite experience. He tried to beat the cost of a U-Haul by buying an old van to move his household goods. He blew three large and expensive tires before a dealer happened to tell him that truck tires need a whole lot more pressure than car tires. Instead of the 80 or 90 pounds per square inch they needed, Dan was running them on heavy-load car pressure: 35 to 40. The flexing and heat was blowing the tires.

Some people can take more pressure than others. Some people *need* pressure to work efficiently. Stress management, the experts say, is not eliminating stress but recognizing some kinds as necessary and some as useless, and then "accentuating the positive."

When faith in Christ is poured into us, it lowers stress and brings peace—because forgiveness comes with it and a comfortable and accepting friend named Jesus.

 Lord, give me the pressure I need to do your work and mine, and the love I need to handle that pressure.

**A friend and I are both under a lot of stress right now. Tomorrow at work I'm going to talk to him about it.**

# ■ HARD TO BELIEVE

Matt. 14:22-33: "You of little faith, . . . why did you doubt?" (v. 31).

Gil Rafferty learned dowsing from a backhoe operator who was looking for an underground septic system with two L-shaped rods in his hands. Every time he crossed over the sewer line or the tank, the rods pulled together. Gil watched incredulously.

After a while the man told Gil he knew just where the line was, and where the tank was too. Gil had some trouble believing.

"Want to try it?" he asked.

"Sure."

Gil took the rods and began walking back and forth. It worked. He could scarcely believe his eyes.

Gil often uses rods or a forked sapling to demonstrate his skill at church camps or at backyard picnics. The sapling will dip down toward underground water, water pipes, or sewer lines. People are almost always skeptical at first. Then Gil simply says, "Try it."

"It really works," they scream. "It's pulling down so hard I can't hold it."

"I told you," Gil says.

Faith is like that. It's hard to have faith in what someone else believes. It's hard to believe that a man who died on a cross 2000 years ago could have an effect on someone's life today. Even though you heard that following Jesus had changed someone's life, it was hard to believe, wasn't it, until you tried it for yourself.

Lord, help me to try my faith and help others try theirs.

**We encourage faith in those who need it and share with those who already have it.**

## ■ PLAYING FOR SCORE

Phil. 3:12-16: "Only let us live up to what we have already attained" (v. 16).

Anyone who has been on a really good team will know the feeling. At some point in the season members of a championship team get a kind of confidence that makes them sure they will win. They are so sure they will win that they start playing for score. They want to score big, to break their school's or even the league's scoring records.

Such a season is rare. What it teaches a team is the exhilaration of assurance, of worrying before a game not *whether* they are going to win, but *by how much*.

A Christian who understands justification and sanctification lives his life like that. Because he understands that Jesus died for him, he knows he is going to win—but he is concerned about the score. He wants to live a high-scoring moral life because it is fun, because God expects it, and because that's one way of thanking God for having him on the team. We call it sanctification.

Lord, help me show how thankful I am just for being on your team by living a high-scoring life.

**The wise Christian knows he can't earn God's love with his morality, but he also knows that morality has its own rewards.**

# ■ HELP FOR LIFE'S WAY

Ps. 78:65-72: "And David shepherded them with integrity of heart; with skillful hand he led them" (v. 72).

In western Canada Ed Hadley was introduced to curling. Curling, Ed observed, is something like bowling, something like shuffleboard except you play on ice with rocks and brooms. You take a 40-pound rock with a handle on top, stick your foot into a notch or "hack" in the ice and then propel that rock toward a target about 100 feet away on the other end of the ice. The captain is down near the target, holding his broom on the ice as a point of aim.

Unlike a bowler, a curler is allowed to slide along with his rock for almost a fourth of the distance. During that slide he guides it, tuning with a feather touch the direction and the speed of the sliding rock.

Even then the rock is not on its own. For the rest of the way toward the target, two and even three teammates can sweep the ice in front of the rock to make it go faster and straighter.

Ed came home thinking that a family and congregation could be compared to a curling team, our lives to a rock. So many people influence our directions and our goals. And even when we think we are on our own, Jesus has always been there, pointing to a spot on target and telling us where he wants us to end up. If we get off course, Christian friends help redirect us and smooth our way.

 Heavenly Father, guide my life in more and more ways. Show me the goals you have set for me.

**If Jesus has not set our aims and our goals, we may be in the wrong game altogether.**

# ■ PUTTING MY FEELINGS TO WORK

Ezek. 22:23-30: "The people of the land practice
extortion and commit robbery; they oppress the poor
and needy . . ." (v. 29).

Sitting through an epic film like *Gandhi* moves us all
through a complex set of feelings. We will side with
the weak when they have courage to stand against
the strong. We will side with the individualist who
has the courage to stand against unjust laws and
unjust leaders.

After such a film we may be embarrassed a bit to
have had tears in our eyes so often, sharing with
Gandhi the death of his wife, the triumphs and
defeats of his complex political career. Walking out of
the theater we are ourselves a complex tangle of
feelings looking for someplace to express themselves.

The church has ways of channeling those feelings:
the thankful feelings we share on Good Friday as the
cross is veiled, the community feelings we share as we
get back to our feet at the communion rail, the
sympathetic feelings that are aroused by a funeral,
the angry or frustrated feelings aroused by a sermon
on injustice, world hunger, or violence.

Sometimes those feelings are the first stirrings of
the Holy Spirit within us, the Spirit trying to motivate
us, to get us into action. If we tune in to those
stirrings, our next move is a phone call, a written and
mailed memo, a short run in the car that will connect
us with a helping professional—a social worker, a
pastor, a chaplain. Our simple question is, "How can I
help?"

✤ Lord, turn my feelings into action.

**A few people endanger their impact by spreading
their help too thin, but most of us are in more danger
of letting the desire to help die away without doing
anything.**

# ■ A BACHELOR AMONG THE KIDS

1 Thess. 2:9-12: "We dealt with each of you as a father deals with his own children" (v. 11).

Arlo liked being single. He was glad his mom and dad hadn't decided that way, but he liked who he was and how his life was working out.

He fixed exotic cars. People who own exotic cars, Arlo learned early on, keep strange hours and might call late at night or on weekends and desperately need work on their Audi, Porsche, Corvette, or BMW. Arlo would work when he had to—day or night.

What bothered him, though, were the kids who hung around the shop. Nothing interests 14-15-year-olds more than exotic cars, and nothing scares the owner of an expensive car more than a teenager hovering near his $1400 paint job.

Arlo was beside himself until he bought the little MG junker. He parked it on the corner of the driveway for the kids to play in and work on. Soon a a couple of them were tinkering with the carburetor and other interior parts, trying to get it running. They asked questions, and Arlo began to see mechanics hiding inside some of those gangly kids.

That's how Valley Auto Club got started, and that's how Arlo became a kind of "father" to a dozen special boys.

 Lord, help me to see the neighborhood kids not as threats but as challenges.

**The youth in every church need help and support. Ask how you can.**

# ■ NOTICING OLDER PEOPLE

Job 12:7-12:   "Is not wisdom found among the aged?" (v. 12).

Rolly had no contact with older people until Martin moved in next door. Rolly's folks were back in the Midwest and pretty much took care of themselves. Besides, his sister lived in their town.

But Martin was his neighbor now, and Martin turned out to be someone special. They began talking over the alley garbage cans, then in the side yard when they raked or mowed. Soon they were going out for coffee and sharing meals. Rolly began to find Martin's experiences and insights unusual and engaging—and often very different from his own.

As he made product decisions for his company in the next few years, Rolly began to think of Martin: Would he use this thing? Would he find the directions difficult to read because of his eyes? Because of Martin, Rolly began to be aware of older people, their concerns, their interests, their weaknesses, and their astounding strengths. He thought of the baby Jesus and Simeon and Anna. He thought of Saul being threatened by young David. He thought of societies even today that respect and revere their elders.

Rolly was glad he had Martin. He hoped they would be neighbors for many years to come.

 Lord, give me at least one older person to know and appreciate and love.

One way of knowing is to help. A call to the church or a volunteer center could turn you into some older person's helping hand.

## ■ SHARING OUR HURTS

Jer. 10:19-20: "Woe to me because of my injury! My wound is incurable!" (v. 19).

Les Wilson's son got his name in the paper, but Les wasn't a bit proud. Ron Wilson's name showed up in the municipal court proceedings column. He was tagged for careless driving.

Les was angry and hurt. Ron had never done anything like that before, and Les didn't know how to handle it. He asked his friend Carl at work:

"Did you see Ron's name in this week's court column?" Les asked.

"No. What did he do?"

"Careless driving. You must be the only one in town who didn't read it."

"Has he done that before?"

"No, first time."

"Well, don't worry. Our Bill was in there four times during high school. He even lost his license. He's settled down now, doing well in college. Don't worry."

Just sharing that common experience helped Les with his anger and frustration. Sharing experiences, sharing hurts, sometimes makes them lighter.

 Lord, help me hear others' hurts and share mine.

**If you are hurting, tell someone. If someone shares a hurt, offer more than sympathy—share your experience.**

# ■ FACING SHORT-TERM LONELINESS

Ps. 25:11-18: "Turn to me and be gracious to me; for I am lonely and afflicted" (v. 16).

When Ralph Winter's wife Becky earned an expense-paid trip to the international conference, he practically busted his buttons telling everyone of her accomplishment.

As the time for her departure grew nearer, Ralph became more and more apprehensive. She would be gone nearly a month, a week for the convention and then some vacation time to visit relatives in the old country. They had never before been apart for more than a day or two.

Ralph's fears were well-founded. Only four or five days after Becky left, he slipped into a funk of loneliness. He moped, he fussed, he paced the floor, he was short with the children (especially when they criticized his cooking).

What tided Ralph over were his friends. One friend called the church, and they set up a loneliness brigade, inviting Ralph and the kids over for dinner, dropping in to sit through the long evenings, calling him on the phone.

As Ralph counted down the last several days of Becky's trip, he thanked God for a wife he loved so much—but he also thanked God for his loving friends.

 Lord, help us to handle our loneliness. Help us also to help others handle theirs.

**Deep loneliness, once experienced, ties us into all of humanity.**

# ■ MALIGNANCY AND FEAR

Psalm 23: "Even though I walk through the valley of the shadow of death . . ." (v. 4).

John Mattigan lay on his back staring at the sterile white ceiling. He had never been so scared in his whole life.

John had lived an almost fear-free life—that is until the past week when the words "suspicious shadow," "biopsy," and "malignant" had moved him from one machine and procedure to another until he found himself in St. Mary's hospital, shaved from neck to knee, and not two hours away from major surgery and the shadow of death.

The chaplain's visits had helped and so had his pastor's, but the aching, haunting fear was still there. It kept him awake, tense, filling him with surprise and shock. He just lay there, trying to squeeze the life out of a fistful of bedsheet with his clammy hands.

What tided him over was thinking of Jesus in Gethsemane, praying to have the cup of death removed, but drinking that cup anyway. John would drink that cup if he had to. Even though he would walk into the shadowy valley, scared to death, he knew he had a Friend on the other side who also knew the apprehension, who also knew the awesome power of death—but who got up off his knees and walked toward it like a lamb.

 We thank you, Lamb of God, for living among us, sharing so much, and pouring your strength into our weakness.

**Jesus did it all—all except the sin. He understands our every thought, our every need, before we even think we need it.**

# ■ FIGHTING DESPAIR

Job 10:1-8:  "I loathe my very life"  (v. 1).

Andy wasn't saying it out loud but he certainly was
thinking it: "Life isn't worth living." He wondered
how down a person could get before he found himself
at a crossroads called suicide. Andy didn't want to
be there—but he knew that once he began to think
life wasn't worth it, he was approaching that juncture.

Even prayer was hard. He had never had such
trouble talking with God. He thought about Job, full
of sores and lamenting on an ash heap. It was as if
God wasn't listening—but he knew better than that.
Silently, from somewhere deep inside, Andy began to
pray a kind of chant: "Lord, show me life. Lord, show
me life."

Suddenly Andy had a vision of death, but not his
own. He saw Jesus on the cross, dying to give him
life. That was the beginning of the way back for
Andy. He begin to see the destructive and despairing
forces in his life and began to ask himself what to do
about them. He decided he had some phone calls to
make and some people to see and some changes to
consider. His life wasn't the greatest right now, but it
wasn't the worst either. With prayer and with help
and with effort things could be better—a whole lot
better.

 Lord, protect me from despair. Make hope my
constant neighbor, the future my friend.

**Friends are a big help in down times. Sometimes we
need them; sometimes they need us.**

# ■ HANDLING SUSPICION

Prov. 3:11-12: "My son, do not despise the Lord's discipline and do not resent his rebuke" (v. 11).

Bill suspected his son Greg of using marijuana. Sometimes when Greg came home at night he had that burning rope smell about him. There were times Bill knew that his suspicions were just that—suspicions —but they ate at him anyway, keeping him awake, and making him irritable and out of sorts.

Bill didn't want to talk to Amy about it either, because she was more of a worrier than he. He prayed regularly about his concerns and suspicions but seemed not to get an answer. Then one day he read in the town paper about a drug-awareness session for concerned parents. That session was the beginning of his answer. Bill learned more about the problem, then armed with both information and concern he began to talk to Greg about his suspicions.

Greg gave him honest answers. Yes, he had done some experimenting, but now he was running with a different crowd and didn't think drugs would be so much of a problem. Bill was relieved—and thankful.

 Lord, give me courage, wisdom, and insight in dealing with my children and their temptations.

**When we don't know where to turn, the Lord sometimes turns the world in our direction.**

# ■ SNAKES ALIVE

Gen. 3:1-13: "The woman said, 'The serpent deceived me, and I ate'" (v. 13).

If you have ever been spooked by a snake, or maybe back in grade school chased by someone with a garter snake, don't feel bad. Among men and women and children, snake phobia has to be one of the most common human fears.

No wonder that the Evil One appears in the temptation story as a snake, and no wonder that the snake has had a bad reputation ever since.

That reputation is mostly undeserved. To be sure, a rattler will strike when surprised or trapped or hurt, but it will escape if it can, and when cornered will at least warn us with hisses and rattles.

We sometimes call people "snakes," "sidewinders," or "vipers," as if a snake were somehow worse than a human, when in fact it is the human alone among God's creatures who often chooses to fight rather than run, who will strike without provocation and without warning.

Our humanness, not our snakelikeness, needs constant watching. Our humanness makes sinners of us all and gave God's Christ a reason to die. The love of God in Christ, and his forgiveness, defangs us daily, gets us off our bellies, and back into life for another try.

 Lord, make me more even-tempered, more predictable and peace-loving.

**In a play about Noah in which people played animals, what creature would your friends and family ask you to play? Would that please you? Would it please God?**

# ■ FORGIVING OTHERS

Matt. 6:7-15: ". . . as we also have forgiven our debtors . . ." (v. 12).

Arlen never thought he could be pushed to such an angry outburst. He had sat there with his two friends and shouted, "I'll never forgive him as long as I live." He was talking about Orv, his brother-in-law, who had refused to come to the wedding.

Sure there had been years of mild blood feud in the family, but Beth's wedding wasn't supposed to become a battleground. Arlen had been hurt plenty of times by the bad blood, but he was devastated to see Beth so hurt. He watched her cry; he tried to comfort her; nothing worked. Watching someone you love being hurt doesn't do much for a forgiving spirit.

He met his friends downtown for coffee next morning and practically everyone in the whole cafe heard his outburst. The friends calmed him down, then took him up to church to see their pastor. They had a long session that Saturday morning. That was the beginning. Orv didn't come to the wedding, but Arlan did forgive him — three years later.

 Lord, make me slower to take offense, quicker to forgive.

**Family feuds are the hardest. We are well advised not to overreact.**

# ■ WHY SHOULD I CARE?

Mark 14:3-9: "The poor you will always have with you, and you can help them anytime you want" (v. 7).

Art walked by the Salvation Army Santa Claus and dropped a quarter in the pot. "That's peanuts," he thought, "considering the work they do. But why should I care? Nobody knocked at my door and offered help when we were kids. We were poor enough."

They were indeed poor enough, and it had been a struggle. Art's mother had stretched and squeezed and worked and made every penny count for 10 years after his dad was killed. Art wondered why she had never remarried. She had had a few chances. He guessed it was her independence.

The feel and the shame of being poor and the anger at having been made poor by sudden death had never really been worked out in Art's mind. He didn't care and yet he did.

Asking "Why should I care?" was inviting the only real answer: "Because I've been there, that's why." Art turned and walked a whole block back to that bell-ringing Santa and put in a ten. Next morning he called his church. "Pastor," he said, "have we any poor family that could use some help?"

That's how he met the Millers, and young Binky Miller. Binky Miller changed Art's life.

 Lord, remind me that changing the world starts with me. Give me the courage to set that change in motion.

**Helping usually needs to be done wisely. The church and some of its agencies often have that wisdom.**

# ■ I'M AFRAID TO SING A SOLO

Psalm 98: "O sing to the Lord a new song . . ." (v. 1).

Walter wanted more than anything in the whole world to sing a solo in church. He didn't want to get praise for it or start on a new career; he just wanted to stand on his own two feet in the balcony next to the organist and raise his voice to God in praise.

This was not an impossible dream. Walter could sing. He had sung in choirs for years, but when any of the directors would say, "Anyone want to try this solo?" Walter would choke up.

Walter went home one summer evening and took a long look at himself in the mirror. "You can sing, you know," he said to his reflection. "You're just afraid, you know," he said. "They wouldn't kill you even if you goofed up, you know."

Walter did a lot of singing that summer. He joined a community summer choir and sang in the shower and sang out in the woods while he was cutting his winter wood supply.

On the first day of school in the autumn, Walter said a quick prayer for courage, then stepped into the kitchen, looked up a number and then dialed. "Is this Mary Larson? The Mary Larson who plays the organ at church . . . ?"

 Lord, help me to see where my true talents are and to use them for your praise and glory.

**Recognizing our abilities is just a beginning. Putting them to work for God's glory is the goal.**

# ■ UNCOVERING OLD GRIEF

2 Cor. 7:8-13: "Godly sorrow brings repentance that leads to salvation and leaves no regret . . ." (v. 10).

On the way home from his therapist's office Gus Steensma kept repeating one word to himself. "Grief," he said, shaking his head. Dr. Kranken had played "20 questions" with Gus, and they had somehow gotten back to a graveside in his hometown nearly five years before.

After everyone else had gone back to church, Gus stood at that graveside — only slightly aware of the two gravediggers over by the fence who were trying not to look impatient. They were waiting to lower and bury his grandmother.

No one in the family could have loved grandma more than Gus. He had lived with her a year and two summers when his father was away to war. Now here he stood, staring at her casket and not feeling much of anything.

Gus was going to learn grief. He would go back to Dr. Kranken once more, then to his pastor for several sessions. He would never really break down and cry, but he would gradually recognize the sadness, the ache, the void inside himself not only for his grandmother, but for a father seldom home and for a life that he wished had been different. The Lord helped Gus confront that grief and helped him to know that life *could* be different.

 Lord, help me uncover the hidden griefs in my earlier life. Then help me get on with the rest of it.

**Identifying that haunting sadness is often the hardest part. Prayer helps. Talking to friends helps, too.**

# ■ INTEGRITY AND LOCAL POLITICS

Matt. 4:8-11: "All this I will give you . . . if you will bow down and worship me" (v. 9).

Craig Huggins had never really asked what it meant to be true to himself until the mayor episode. Several local businessmen who were active in city politics came over one night and asked Craig to run. He was well-known around town; he was active in one of the larger churches, and his family had run a clothing store in town for three generations. There were plenty of people in a hundred-mile radius of that little city who knew the name Huggins.

Craig had thought some about city politics. There were some things that needed changing. He thought particularly about the municipal court system, the police force, and the high property taxes that made it even harder for young couples to buy homes.

What frightened him was that his supporters were investors: condominium and shopping-center types who wanted to control city government for their own profit. They thought the Huggins name would swing it.

Craig thought and prayed about it for two weeks. He finally decided not to run for mayor but to try organizing a citizen's committee to work on his reforms. Trying to do good by going against his own integrity and beliefs was not God's way.

Lord, help us not to consort with evil in our attempts to do good.

**Recognizing negative pressure groups in local politics often makes us reevaluate some of our friendships and business associations.**

# ■ CELEBRATING AN OLD FRIEND

Prov. 18:24: "There is a friend who sticks closer than a brother."

Martin Jennings and Eric Mason had been friends for 40 years. They became fast friends in junior high school, and apart from a few youthful tiffs have been friends ever since.

Eric sat in his office one noon and mused over that friendship. He recognized how blessed he was in having such a trusted and long-term friend as Martin, and then and there he bowed and thanked God for that blessing.

But Eric wanted to do more than thank God; he wanted to thank Martin also. He called a few other mutual friends and invited them to a surprise friendship party for Martin. The party was a special kind of success. They reminisced through the whole evening, and for once all these old friends opened up and thanked each other for the faithful friendships. At several points there were tears in their eyes.

We should all be so blessed as Martin and Eric were in having enjoyed a four-decade friendship. We should all be so courageous as to tell our friends how much we love and appreciate them.

 Lord, make me thankful for my friends — and give me the courage to say so.

**Being able to enjoy long-term friendships when we are older often depends upon how we choose friends when we are younger.**

# ■ HANDLING A PEST

Luke 18:1-8: "Because this widow keeps bothering me, I will see that she gets justice, so that she won't eventually wear me out with her coming!" (v. 5).

The parable is about prayer — but there are other lessons. When Norman Nagel heard this parable read in church, he thought back to high school and the strange friendship he had with Herbert Gervaise. Herb moved to town in the spring of their junior year and was never really accepted by any of the groups. He wasn't an athlete or a musician; he wasn't quick-witted or outgoing; he just didn't fit in.

Norm moved pretty freely among the groups in his school. He was in choir and played basketball and was on student council. But it was youth group that connected him with Herb. They discussed school cliques and outsiders one Sunday night, and the very next day Norm began to talk to Herb.

Herb really latched on. He followed Norm everywhere that spring, called him once or twice a night, and always acted hurt when Herb did things with other friends. Sometimes Norm wanted to scream —or to move to a different town. Norm did bring him to youth group, though, and there Herb began to make other friends. By the middle of their senior year, Norm and Herb were more casual friends.

Norm got a letter from Herb 10 years later thanking him for his unselfish friendship at a very lonely time. It is one of the few letters Norm has saved.

Lord, make me sensitive to others' loneliness. Make me an unselfish friend.

**Loneliness is the supreme pain. When you see it around you, take a risk and do something about it.**

# ■ SETTING PRIORITIES

Luke 18:18-30: "Peter said to him, 'We have left all we had to follow you!'" (v. 28).

Paul Deitz nursed his car into the wheel-alignment shop. The front end was shaking terribly. "Sounds like you threw a wheel weight," the man said. "Let's look." He bent over the front wheel, then pointed. "There. Looks like you rubbed it off on a curb." In less than 15 minutes the wheel was off, rebalanced, and back on Paul's car.

As he drove away, Paul reflected that balancing his life wasn't nearly that easy. Since he had been elected president of the church council, he was having trouble with priorities. He was spending several nights a week with committees at church, and just at the time when his kids seemed to need him more— and his wife, too. He certainly shouldn't neglect his work either, just when the boss was beginning to treat him like someone special.

Paul plugged this concern into his regular prayers, and he talked to Katie about it, too. What he learned was to delegate authority. There were sensible, responsible people on every committee. Sometimes calling someone on the committee the next day or asking for a written report was enough.

St. Peter may have given up his home life to follow Jesus those several years, but Jesus didn't seem to be asking that of Paul Deitz — especially not to do busy work.

Lord, help me see the real priorities in my life and empower me to make them work that way.

**Learning the distinction between real involvement and mere activity is often the beginning of good stewardship of time.**

# ■ MAKING EXCUSES

Luke 14:15-24: "A certain man was preparing a great banquet and invited many guests . . . but they all alike began to make excuses" (vv. 16, 18).

We make excuses for those things we know we should do but don't want to do. No one bothers to make excuses for those things he hates and thinks unnecessary: "Come on and join the sky-diving club with me."

"Are you kidding? Even with an angel on either arm I'd never jump out of an airplane." No excuses, no nonsense, no runaround — just *no*.

It's different when someone calls and says, "Let's go to the concert tonight." Down deep you know you should be more supportive of the arts in town, and you've been telling yourself to be a bit more cultured. So you say, "I'd like to, but I have this report to do for the company." It isn't a lie exactly; you do have a report to do — but it isn't due for 10 days.

When we are asked to do things for the church, it's harder yet: teach Sunday school? be on a committee? join the choir? We make excuses.

But the hardest of all is facing up to the demands of our inner voices: "Why don't you pray more?" "Why don't you go to church more regularly?" "Why don't you be a better Christian — invite your neighbor to church, visit the sick and shut-in?" Unfortunately, the excuses we make to ourselves are the hardest to believe.

 Lord, make me more willing and more able to bear the fruits of my Christian faith.

**Maybe swearing off excuses would help set priorities and lead to a healthier involvement in church and community.**

# ■ MY MIND WANDERS IN CHURCH

2 Peter 1:16-21: "We ourselves heard this voice that came from heaven when we were with him on the sacred mountain (v. 18).

With him on the sacred mountain" was the phrase that set Irwin Crawford's mind off on a reverie during the sermon. His mind often wandered in church, starting out with an idea in a hymn or a lesson or the sermon. "I wonder if it's a sin not to listen more carefully," he often thought.

This time the words "on the sacred mountain" brought to mind a vision of Irwin himself and Jesus on a mountain climb. Irwin was deathly afraid of heights, but in the theater of his mind he could see Jesus with brightly colored ropes and a hammer and those little pitons or whatever they were called. And Jesus was hammering those eyelets into the mountain and confidently snapping on rings and hooking up ropes. Jesus always went ahead, always went up first.

Irwin saw himself as completely unafraid on that climb. "Who could fall with Jesus . . . fastening in the ropes?" he thought.

Suddenly the congregation was singing a hymn. The sermon was over. He had altogether lost the last five minutes. He determined to listen more carefully next week, but he also said to himself, "Maybe God speaks even to my wandering mind. Maybe mountain climbing with Jesus was what I should have been doing this morning." He opened his hymnbook and began to sing — a bit more confidently than usual.

Lord Jesus, lead my wandering mind into your pathways, your visions, your insights.

**Spiritual concentration is indeed good, but dreams and visions and visitations are also very important in the Bible.**

# ■ KEEPING THE MIND FRESH

Rom. 12:1-2: "Be transformed by the renewing of your mind" (v. 2).

When Keith sat there in church and heard Mrs. Atwood reading the lesson from Romans, what stuck in his mind was the phrase, "the renewing of your mind." He had been writing music for the same advertising agency for five years, and he knew that doing television commercials that long for the same company was like an eternity.

What was getting him lately was what some of his colleagues and his competitors and even a few of his friends were saying about his work — things like, "You did the music for the Glisten commercial, didn't you? I thought so. I recognized your style." Keith knew he was sliding downhill and out of control when all his stuff sounded alike. His mind was stale; his creativity was at a standstill.

"A renewing of my mind, that's what I need," he thought. His mind went back to a bulletin announcement. He looked again. "Sign up now for the singles renewal weekend," it said. He thought that would be different enough. Maybe there he would find renewal.

On that retreat Keith met Barbara. She taught private music lessons and was an expert on medieval madrigals. From those tunes and from Barbara, Keith was soon composing in an entirely new style. He and Barbara were finding other harmonies, too.

Lord, show me where inspiration may lie.
Make me open to it.

**Often creative renewal is as close as the telephone and as available as the grace of God.**

## ■ SIBLING UNREST

Gen. 27:30-36: "Esau said, 'Isn't he rightly named Jacob [the deceiver, the usurper]? He has deceived me these two times: He took my birthright, and now he's taken my blessing!' " (v. 36).

Jacob did it to him twice. Some brothers are like that. They fight and fight and one somehow manages to cheat the other again and again. We shouldn't be surprised at Jacob and Esau. Those twins are reported to have had their first fight in Rebekah's womb.

Sibling rivalry was a fact way before Freud. Look at Cain and Abel, Jacob and Esau, and Joseph and his brothers. These stories are also similar in involving competition for the father's blessing and affection and love.

Unrelated people are constantly at odds for many reasons, but they seldom achieve the depths of bitterness that feuding siblings do. One brother gets the farm and the others are jealous. They end up in court. One child inherits the best heirlooms and the others resent it. They quit coming to family reunions. One sister's kids seem to get all the affection and love of their grandparents. The children become pawns in the rivalry.

The submissive Christ won by losing. His love survived all the treachery and betrayal and misunderstanding and cruelty. Love is what finally survives in troubled families, too—but almost always in slow and subtle ways.

Lord, make me my brother's keeper and my brother's friend — and my sister's, too.

**Those few family members who keep positive attitudes can often rescue the whole clan before it drowns in its own hatred.**

# ■ A TRICKY FATHER-IN-LAW

Gen. 29:15-30: "Jacob was in love with Rachel and said, 'I'll work for you seven years in return for your younger daughter Rachel' " (v. 18).

After what Jacob and his mother did to blind Isaac and brother Esau, maybe God owed him a father-in-law like Laban. Laban and Jacob tricked and schemed against each other for 20 years. Jacob worked 14 of those years to get the wife he really wanted, and for six more years his wage was all the spotted sheep. Laban meanwhile sent every spotted lamb away to his sons. But the Lord blessed Jacob anyway, and Jacob and Laban finally parted with a friendly covenant.

Sometimes we don't get along quite so well with our in-laws. Sometimes we hassle and jockey for position and disagree over whether the woman in question is a wife or still a daughter. The relationships can get pretty sticky.

But time can heal many things. Jacob and Laban, for all their tricks and deceits, parted friends. For a moving postscript to this story, read on in Genesis 32 and 33 to see how Jacob and Esau were restored 20 years after those youthful run-ins.

Time and love and prayer can restore relationships in our families too, if we give them half a chance.

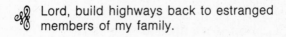 Lord, build highways back to estranged members of my family.

**Jacob and Laban could have been restored sooner if either one had quit paying back trick for trick.**

# ■ CULTIVATING PATIENCE

Luke 2:22-35: "Now there was a man in Jerusalem called Simeon, who was righteous and devout. He was looking for the consolation of Israel" (v. 25).

Patience is a virtue" they say, but few of us believe it. A great deal of both good and bad in this world and in our own lives is a result of impatience. Impatient drivers, especially young ones, are second only to drinking drivers in their danger to themselves and to others. Impatient farmers who plant or harvest early often lose their gambles. Impatient parents can push their children into mental breakdowns by rushing their development. Impatient suitors may lose the very objects of their love by looking too soon for too much response.

But impatience has also been the father of much progress and technological development. Edison was impatient with the darkness, Ford with the horse and buggy, the Wright brothers with being earthbound.

Some of the best things are slow in coming, though, and patience can indeed be a virtue. God's promised Messiah was slow in coming, and Simeon had a long wait. It takes a long time for our faith to polish our Christian lives into any kind of maturity. Building the life of faith means trusting God's grace to give us patience and persistence and the stubborn will to try again and again and again when we falter or fail or fall.

 Lord, teach me when to be patient and when to be impatient, when to hang back and when to be out and doing.

**Overstressing patience or impatience in life may actually be clouding our judgment and decisions.**

# ■ THE GRANDCHILD OF AN ALCOHOLIC

Gen. 9:20-25: "When Noah awoke from his wine and found out what his youngest son had done to him, he said, 'Cursed be Canaan . . .' " (v. 24).

You've seen it happen. The children and even grandchildren of problem drinkers and other ill and disturbed persons suffer from broken marriages, injuries, crimes, and venereal disease that might not have happened were it not for misplaced anger and mental frustration made worse by alcohol or drugs. It is not only a modern problem.

Ham, the youngest of Noah's three sons, happened in on his drunken father lying naked in his tent. That broke an ancient modesty and incest taboo that prohibited children from seeing their parents naked.

Surprisingly, Ham himself was not punished. Noah's drunkenness and Ham's mistake resulted in a curse on *Canaan,* Ham's *son.* That seems like unfairness beyond belief.

Life has never been fair to children. Because they are so powerless, they are disinherited, neglected, aborted, and abused by adults — and the problem moves from generation to generation (Exod. 20:5). As Christian men we can be constantly ready to use our wisdom, our strength, our positions, and our political clout to protect all children from all hurt.

Lord, make me more aware of the needs of all children — especially my own.

A plan, an actual "mode of operation" for spending good time with children, has been helpful to many parents.

# ■ THANK GOD FOR MY WIFE

Judg. 13:21-25: "But his wife said to him, 'If the Lord had meant to kill us, he would not have accepted a burnt offering . . .'" (v. 23).

Manoah must have thanked God again and again for his wife. With this wise woman he shared the special privilege of raising their chosen child, Samson. Her wisdom and insight and acceptance of God's will are shown in her reaction to the visit of God's angel.

How often we ought to thank God if we have married well. Particularly after weathering some years of the thick and thin of marriage, we sometimes shake our heads and wonder how we could have been so blessed. No one but God could have engineered such a fortunate meeting of boy and girl and resulted in this marriage, this family, this love. When we were so young, teenagers even, God somehow crossed our paths, gave us love, and brought us together.

Young love is exciting, heady, and impulsive, but the mature love of husband and wife is cherished like the pearl of great price. Hardly any happily married man or woman would go back to that unsure, flighty, emotionally jarring time of young romance. Marriage, like an apple, makes the caring hand of God most apparent in ripeness.

 Thank you, Lord, for my wife, my precious friend and partner and lover.

**It is good to thank God for a loving wife; it is good as well to thank your wife for also loving God.**

# ■ GIVING TIME TO A CHILD

Josh. 4:19-24:  "In the future when your
descendants ask their fathers, 'What do these stones
mean?' tell them . . . " (vv. 21-22).

Divorced fathers are better fathers. Tragic but true.
Maybe they aren't better than all other fathers, but
usually they are better fathers *than they were*. When
a court of law tells a father who has lost custody of
his children, "You will have thus many hours on such
and such days," he suddenly begins to plan some
quality time with his children.

The problem is that we are often the poorest fathers
when our opportunities are the greatest. When we
are at home, together with our families and have all
the time in the world, we often choose to use little
or none of it for our children. That is a tragic truth.

One remarkable characteristic of the early Israelites
was how they taught the truths, father to children,
down through the generations. "What do these stones
mean?" was a deadly serious question to a Hebrew
father.

Martin Luther, too, saw the father's role as primary
in religious training. Luther introduced the *Small
Catechism* in this way: "In the plain form in which
fathers should teach it to their children."

For such important interaction we should have all
the time in the world. Shouldn't we?

 Lord, help me to take more good time with my
children and to use some of it to teach them
about you.

It shouldn't take a fractured marriage and a court
order to force me to set aside a *certain, specified* time
for my children.

# ■ I'M A MAN NOW, MOTHER

John 2:1-11: "Dear woman, why do you involve me?" (v. 4).

It may help to know that Jesus had the same problem: a meddling mother. Who can stop a mother from caring and trying to guide the life of her child? And why should Jesus' mother be any different?

Jesus was a late bloomer by first-century standards. The angels and the dreams promised Mary and Joseph an important religious person in their son—but at age 30 he was only just getting started. His mother may have pushed him and nagged him a bit in the third decade of his life.

But when Jesus walked out of the Jordan, baptized and ready for his work, he had to set limits on family involvement in his ministry. The wedding at Cana was the beginning of the end. He was sharp with her not only there but also when she and the family came to him in Galilee.

We all need to establish adult relationships with our parents at some point. Some of us put it off too long. In some tragic cases a son becomes his mother's keeper and loses all opportunity for romance, marriage, and independence. Her selfishness and his overconcern for her loneliness will only insure his own utter loneliness later on.

 Lord, help me to love my parents with wise moderation.

**For the overmothered young man sometimes relocation is the only answer. Space can sometimes reshape relationships, sometimes for the better.**

# ■ THE IMMOVABLE FATHER

2 Sam. 19:31-38: "Let your servant return, that I may die in my own town near the tomb of my father and mother" (v. 37).

Most older people like to stay in comfortable and familiar spaces. Eighty-year-old Borzilai, King David's friend, was that way. So was Michael Mantel's father. When Mike decided at last that his father should no longer live alone, he called all the retirement centers around the area. There were openings in a couple of pretty nice places. But he knew he was going to have a fight on his hands.

Before he even mentioned his plan to his father, Mike prayed about the situation. The answer came quickly and came to him in church. There he met a young couple from the college. They had three more years to go and were looking for cheap housing.

"How would you like to live with a crochety old man only four blocks from campus?" Mike asked.

In two weeks it was all set. Mike's father would stay home for three more years at least and probably would perk up considerably having someone else in the house once again.

 Lord, as we have to deal with our aging parents, give us wisdom and patience, and openness to different courses of action.

There are so many options for older people today. Talk to a social worker, the county or city health office, your pastor, and anyone else you can think of before fixing on any one choice.

# ■ THE SPORTS NUT

Luke 12:16-21:  "And I'll say to myself, 'You have plenty of good things laid up for many years'" (v. 19).

Alex Olson was a sports nut. He did everything he could in athletics and did several things quite well. He skied well on both water and snow. He was the catcher and leading hitter on the church softball team and was among the two or three best raquetball players in town.

Doing these things wasn't enough, though. Alex had to try everything. He played tennis, he ran in local marathons, he joined a summer soccer league, and, until he hurt his shoulder, he played rugby in the autumn.

When Alex wasn't participating in sports he was watching them on TV or reading the sports page.

One day in church the pastor preached about the foolish farmer and called him a one-dimensional person. Alex had been feeling vaguely uneasy about all his sports activities, and that phrase did it to him. He was too one-dimensional. "My second love has always been the church," he thought. "Maybe I could do some dropping and adding of activities. Maybe I could start investing some of my time."

 Lord, guard me against being too one-dimensional. Help me to see clearly how I am really investing the precious time you have given me.

**In a world of so many great ideas and interesting people, it is too bad to be stuck in one cubbyhole.**

# ■ LEARNING FROM THE MOVIES

Luke 23:44-49: "Surely this was a righteous man" (v. 47).

Most of us have had too much of our image of manhood carved out by Hollywood, the television industry, and Madison Avenue advertisers. In the computer banks of our minds, manhood is a confusing mixture of weird media images. We are taught early on to see ourselves with hair glistening after a Sudso shampoo, teeth gleaming from a brushing with Glisten, hands cleaner than usual with Sandoff: The Mechanic's Soap. We are wearing Kalvin Klinger jeans, Beaver boots, and of course Heinz underwear. The picture wouldn't be complete without a Carcino cigarette in one hand and a glass of Z and Z scotch in the other.

Our times aren't easy, either, when even the traditional *macho* measurements of manhood are disappearing. How many cords of wood can you split in a day? How straight a furrow can you plow? How many sheep can you shear? How straight can you shoot?

Manhood has lost a measurement as breadwinner, too, with well over half the wives working and often at jobs that used to be called "man's work."

So how do we measure manhood? We Christians can and probably should measure ourselves against the image of Jesus, who was faithful to his friends, a friend to anyone and everyone, helpful and concerned, and finally sacrificial in his devotion to others. The picture of Jesus hanging on the cross is, finally and fully, the measure of man.

Lord, help me to measure my manhood in meaningful ways, ways pleasing to you.

**Often the ways we think we outwardly show our manhood mask our inner insecurities and uncertainties.**

# ■ BIG BOYS DON'T CRY

Luke 22:54-62: "And he went outside and wept bitterly" (v. 62).

Del can remember his father saying dozens of times, "Big boys don't cry." He believed it. Not crying became an article of his manly creed and stayed that way until his daughter was injured in a car-bicycle accident. She was unconscious for eight days. On the sixth day he was watching her lying there connected to all the tubes and contraptions, worrying, and praying, when suddenly it all overwhelmed Del. He began to cry.

His wife sat with him in the parents' room, comforting him. "I've never done this before," he said. "I haven't cried since I was a kid."

"I know," his wife said, "and it's about time you did."

Del decided maybe she was right. He felt better after crying, released and relaxed. He decided that the injury and his daughter's unconsciousness were in the hands of the Lord and the medical team. He continued to pray.

Two days later his daughter woke up and soon was home and back to normal. After that day in the hospital, Del often found tears in his eyes at concerts, movies, and when touched by sympathy for others. Del never said to his own sons, "Big boys don't cry."

 Lord, enrich my emotional life. Help me to feel the experience of living this life very deeply—and to express those feelings.

**Those men who are able to cry under strong impetus are often the same ones who laugh easily and well.**

# ■ SOME TENSION IS OK

Phil. 4:4-7: "Do not be anxious about anything, but in everything, by prayer and petition with thanksgiving, present your requests to God" (v. 6).

Was Jesus exaggerating, or what? It is as impossible for us to be without anxiety as it is to be perfect. Anxiety is even desirable sometimes. We remember that Jesus was quite upset with Peter and the others in the Garden of Gethsemane when they went to sleep and didn't share that night with him.

Where then is the balance? We all have friends and relatives who have died of anxiety, the Type A persons who have worked and worried themselves to death.

Maybe it is simply a controlled level of caring— caring about others, caring enough to do a job well, caring enough that we have thought of all the angles when our committee makes a decision, caring enough about our employer to meet deadlines, to go the second mile when necessary.

That is the same kind of caring that should keep us awake when we know that our Lord and Savior is up on a hillside sweating out the doubts and temptations of his last night on earth. Peter and the others didn't know that. We do. Knowing and understanding and sharing and caring produce tension. Some tension is OK.

 Lord, keep me buoyed up for the important things; drown my needless and negative anxieties.

**Finding the ideal tension level is not easy. Through prayer, self-examination, and seeking wise counsel we can sometimes get close.**

# ■ SHARING HOUSEHOLD DUTIES

Eccles. 4:9-12: "Two are better than one, because they have a good return for their work" (v. 9).

Did you read about the housewife who went on strike?" Daniel shouted out to the kitchen.

"You bet I did," Martha shouted back toward his easy chair, "and I'm considering it."

"Aw, come on, Martha. It isn't that bad."

"Have you ever figured out how much time you spend working around the house and how much time I spend?"

"Not really. But we do different things. I mow and shovel and fix stuff."

"Yes, and I wash and cook and clean. Let's just talk about hours."

"Well, OK, maybe we should."

"How about this week? What have you done?"

"Well, I ah. . . . Well, ah. . . ."

"See? It was different before I started to work. When you worked and the kids were home I didn't complain. I don't even complain now. But now we're both working full-time."

"I know, you're right. But you wouldn't want to eat my cooking, would you?"

"Sure I would, sometimes. I certainly wouldn't mind eating off dishes you washed or using a bathroom you'd cleaned."

"Well, Martha, he did say a partnership, didn't he?"

"Who?"

"The pastor, when we got married. Got a dry dish towel?"

Lord, let me sometimes see our partnership with my wife's eyes.

No marriage partnership is exactly 50/50, but we ought to try for as much fairness, in love, as we can achieve.

# ■ ORGANIZING TO HELP AT HOME

Luke 10:38-42: "Lord, don't you care that my sister has left me to do the work by myself? Tell her to help me!" (v. 40).

The Saturday morning list appeared on the refrigerator door like the famous handwriting on the wall or like Luther's 95 Theses. The handwriting this time was Martha's:

| | |
|---|---|
| MOM: | Clean refrigerator, wash kitchen floor, make lunch |
| DAD: | Clean downstairs bathroom, dust *everywhere* |
| PETER: | Clean room, vacuum downstairs |
| SIS: | Sweep upstairs hallway and stairs, wash front entryway floor |

"Is this some kind of ultimatum?" Daniel asked.

"No, I'm just organizing the partnership we talked about," Martha replied.

"What if I refuse?" Dan asked, with a twinkle in his eye.

"Then our kids will grow up like you grew up, thinking a mother is some kind of slave or servant."

"I never really believed that."

"But you acted like you did. Shouldn't our kids learn partnership early?" Martha knew she had him there.

"I can't possibly dust everywhere," Daniel said, snapping at her playfully with the dust rag.

"I mean everywhere in this house."

Lord, make me a useful member of the family team in our household partnership.

**Husband and wife must *both* agree to parcel out duties also to the children and see that they get done.**

# ■ A FRIEND YOU CAN TRUST

John 15:12-17:   "Instead, I have called you friends"
(v. 15).

There are a lot of ways of being a friend. As we all
look back over the years of our friendships, we can
probably see our friends getting fewer in number,
our friendships getting stronger and their interactions
getting more caring and useful.

Young people often measure themselves and others
by the sheer numbers of their friendships. The more
friends the better. Recent psychological studies
suggest that having from three to five close friends
is ideal and that one of those closest friends should
also be a "bosom buddy," someone with whom we can
be especially open and honest.

Most of us don't choose that nearest friend
consciously; the friendship develops. The person
somehow is just there for years and even decades and
at some point of need — their need or ours — both
recognize that this is one of those special friendships.

Jesus was that sort of friend when he walked this
earth. What was unique in him was that he could
usually establish long-term trust instantly. He still can.
Including him in our list of closest and most trusted
friends makes us blessed indeed.

 Lord Jesus, you are my friend in need. Help me
to recognize that other friend I need—and who
also needs me.

**To make friends is to be vulnerable. There is no such
thing as a no-risk friendship.**